Clear**Revise**

AQA GCSE
Geography 8035

Illustrated revision and practice

Published by
PG Online Limited
The Old Coach House
35 Main Road
Tolpuddle
Dorset
DT2 7EW
United Kingdom

sales@pgonline.co.uk
www.pgonline.co.uk
2022

PG ONLINE

PREFACE

Absolute clarity! That's the aim.

This is everything you need to ace the examined component in this course and beam with pride. Each topic is laid out in a beautifully illustrated format that is clear, approachable and as concise and simple as possible.

Each section of the specification is clearly indicated to help you cross-reference your revision. The checklist on the contents pages will help you keep track of what you have already worked through and what's left before the big day.

We have included worked exam-style questions with answers for almost every topic. This helps you understand where marks are coming from and to see the theory at work for yourself in an exam situation. There is also a set of exam-style questions at the end of each section for you to practise writing answers for. You can check your answers against those given at the end of the book.

LEVELS OF LEARNING

Based on the degree to which you are able to truly understand a new topic, we recommend that you work in stages. Start by reading a short explanation of something, then try and recall what you've just read. This has limited effect if you stop there but it aids the next stage. Question everything. Write down your own summary and then complete and mark a related exam-style question. Cover up the answers if necessary but learn from them once you've seen them. Lastly, teach someone else. Explain the topic in a way that they can understand. Have a go at the different practice questions – they offer an insight into how and where marks are awarded.

Design and artwork: Jessica Webb and Mike Bloys / PG Online Ltd

First edition 2022 10 9 8 7 6 5 4 3 2 1
A catalogue entry for this book is available from the British Library
ISBN: 978-1-910523-30-8
Contributors: Catherine Owen and Jacob Profitt
Copyright © PG Online 2022 All rights reserved.

THE SCIENCE OF REVISION

Illustrations and words

Research has shown that revising with words and pictures doubles the quality of responses by students.[1] This is known as 'dual-coding' because it provides two ways of fetching the information from our brain. The improvement in responses is particularly apparent in students when they are asked to apply their knowledge to different problems. Recall, application and judgement are all specifically and carefully assessed in public examination questions.

Retrieval of information

Retrieval practice encourages students to come up with answers to questions.[2] The closer the question is to one you might see in a real examination, the better. Also, the closer the environment in which a student revises is to the 'examination environment', the better. Students who had a test 2–7 days away did 30% better using retrieval practice than students who simply read, or repeatedly reread material. Students who were expected to teach the content to someone else after their revision period did better still.[3] What was found to be most interesting in other studies is that students using retrieval methods and testing for revision were also more resilient to the introduction of stress.[4]

Ebbinghaus' forgetting curve and spaced learning

Ebbinghaus' 140-year-old study examined the rate at which we forget things over time. The findings still hold true. However, the act of forgetting facts and techniques, and relearning them is what cements them into the brain.[5] Spacing out revision is more effective than cramming – we know that, but students should also know that the space between revisiting material should vary depending on how far away the examination is. A cyclical approach is required. An examination 12 months away necessitates revisiting covered material about once a month. A test in 30 days should have topics revisited every 3 days – intervals of roughly a tenth of the time available.[6]

Summary

Students: the more tests and past questions you do, in an environment as close to examination conditions as possible, the better you are likely to perform on the day. If you prefer to listen to music while you revise, tunes without lyrics will be far less detrimental to your memory and retention. Silence is most effective.[5] If you choose to study with friends, choose carefully – effort is contagious.[7]

1.   Mayer, R. E., & Anderson, R. B. (1991). Animations need narrations: An experimental test of dual-coding hypothesis. *Journal of Education Psychology*, (83)4, 484–490.

2.   Roediger III, H. L., & Karpicke, J.D. (2006). Test-enhanced learning: Taking memory tests improves long-term retention. *Psychological Science*, 17(3), 249–255.

3.   Nestojko, J., Bui, D., Kornell, N. & Bjork, E. (2014). Expecting to teach enhances learning and organisation of knowledge in free recall of text passages. *Memory and Cognition*, 42(7), 1038–1048.

4.   Smith, A. M., Floerke, V. A., & Thomas, A. K. (2016) Retrieval practice protects memory against acute stress. *Science*, 354(6315), 1046–1048.

5.   Perham, N., & Currie, H. (2014). Does listening to preferred music improve comprehension performance? *Applied Cognitive Psychology*, 28(2), 279–284.

6.   Cepeda, N. J., Vul, E., Rohrer, D., Wixted, J. T. & Pashler, H. (2008). Spacing effects in learning a temporal ridgeline of optimal retention. *Psychological Science*, 19(11), 1095–1102.

7.   Busch, B. & Watson, E. (2019), *The Science of Learning*, 1st ed. Routledge.

ACKNOWLEDGEMENTS

The questions in the ClearRevise textbook are the sole responsibility of the authors and have neither been provided nor approved by the examination board.

Every effort has been made to trace and acknowledge ownership of copyright. The publishers will be happy to make any future amendments with copyright owners that it has not been possible to contact. The publisher would like to thank the following companies and individuals who granted permission for the use of their images in this textbook.

Graphics / images: © Shutterstock
Kilauea volcano © Fredy Thuerig / Shutterstock
Loading supplies, Antigua © Lucy.Brown / Shutterstock
Typhoon Haiyan © ymphotos / Shutterstock
Cyclone shelter © PradeepGaurs / Shutterstock
Global temperature graph NOAA Climate.gov
Inuit man and child © Ruben M Ramos / Shutterstock
Svalbard plane © Fasttailwind / Shutterstock.com
Lagos aerial view © Tayvay / Shutterstock.com
Mokoko, Lagos © Dan Ikpoyi / Shutterstock.com
Tuk tuk © UnsulliedBokeh / Shutterstock.com
Carnival © Stephen Maudsley / Shutterstock.com
London traffic © Brian Minkoff / Shutterstock.com
Windermere © Nigel Jarvis / Shutterstock
Waterfall © Kev Gregory / Shutterstock.com
Factory workers © humphery / Shutterstock.com
Fairtrade bananas © Thinglass / Shutterstock.com
Kigali © Stephanie Braconnier / Shutterstock.com
Kigali Marriott © Andreas Marquardt / Shutterstock.com
Operation © Tayvay / Shutterstock.com
Chiswick Park © William Barton / Shutterstock.com
Cambourne © Munyati Nur / Shutterstock.com
Heathrow protest © Dinendra Haria / Shutterstock.com
Port Liverpool © Ivan Kuzkin / Shutterstock.com
Carrying water © Marius Dobilas / Shutterstock.com
World Bank © Andriy Blokhin / Shutterstock.com
China's South-North Project By Nsbdgc CC BY-SA 4.0
Maps on pages 69, 93 and 125 © Crown copyright and database rights 2022 OS 100065506

Warming stripes WMO, 1850–2018 - Climate Lab Book, Ed Hawkins
Nepal quake damage © Suttisak Soralump
Kenyan sand dam © The Water Project
Hurricane Sandy © MISHELLA / Shutterstock
Dredging River Frome © Nigel Jarvis / Shutterstock
Lake District © 365_visuals / Shutterstock
Engine shed views © Jon Rowley
Hydrograph, CC BY, Steven Heath
Lekki Ikoyi Bridge © ariyo olasunkanmi / Shutterstock.com
Ajegunle City, Lagos © Tayvay / Shutterstock.com
Traffic © Santos Akhilele Aburime / Shutterstock.com
Temple Meads Station © N.M.Bear / Shutterstock.com
Rainforest and Bristol images © G & C Owen Bowness on
Kathmandu refugee camp © Salvacampillo / Shutterstock.com
Windrush protest © David Mbiyu / Shutterstock.com
Jubilee for Climate © Loredana Sangiuliano / Shutterstock.com
Irrigation system © BOULENGER Xavier / Shutterstock.com
Loan collection © NEERAZ CHATURVEDI / Shutterstock.com
Shell Plc sign © josefkubes / Shutterstock.com
Business park © salarko / Shutterstock.com
Cambridge Science Park © DrimaFilm / Shutterstock.com
HS2 signage © Alex Daniels / Shutterstock.com
Wirral waterfront © Philip Brookes / Shutterstock.com
Environment Agency van © Andrew Harker / Shutterstock.com
Desalination plant © Stanislav71 / Shutterstock.com
Potteries, 'Stoke on Trent © RMC42 / Shutterstock.com

CONTENTS

Paper 1   Living with the physical environment

Section A   The challenge of natural hazards

Section B   The living world

Paper 2 Challenges in the human environment
Section A Urban issues and challenges

Section B   The changing economic world

☑

Section C   The challenge of resource management

☑

MARK ALLOCATIONS

Green mark allocations[1] on answers to in-text questions through this guide help to indicate where marks are gained within the answers. A bracketed '1' e.g. [1] = one valid point worthy of a mark. There are often many more points to make than there are marks available so you have more opportunity to max out your answers than you may think.

Higher mark questions require extended responses. Marks are not given as the answers should be marked as a whole in accordance with the levels of response guidance on **pages 178-179**.

TOPICS FOR PAPER 1

Living with the physical environment

Information about Paper 1

Written exam: 1 hour 30 minutes
88 marks (including 3 marks for spelling, punctuation, grammar and specialist terminology (SPaG). SPaG will only be assessed in a single extended response question where indicated).

Section A: All questions are mandatory (33 marks)
Section B: All questions are mandatory (25 marks)
Section C: Answer any two questions (30 marks)

Option of earthquakes or volcanoes in Q1
Option of hot deserts or cold environments in Q2
Two options from river landscapes in the UK, coastal landscapes in the UK, and glacial landscapes in the UK.

35% of qualification grade

Specification coverage

The challenge of natural hazards, the living world, physical landscapes in the UK, geographical skills.

The content for this assessment will be drawn from the essential subject content in sections 3.1.1–3.1.3 and 3.4 of the specification.

Questions

A mix of multiple-choice, short answer and extended-writing questions assessing knowledge, understanding and skills in contextual scenarios.

NATURAL HAZARDS

Natural hazards are events which can pose a major risk to humanity. When natural hazards occur close to human populations, there is a significant risk that there may be loss of life, damage to property and impacts on the quality of life.

Types of natural hazard

Earthquake

Wildfire

Tropical storm

Tsunami

Volcano

Factors affecting hazard risk

It is important that **hazard risk** (the probability and chance of natural hazards impacting humans) is fully understood, so that they can be managed effectively. The following factors increase the risk from natural hazards:

Development

The standard of living and quality of life in an area will impact hazard risk. Areas with lower levels of development (LICs/NEEs) will potentially be less prepared for a hazard event than an area with higher levels of development (HICs).

Urbanisation

Urban areas, such as towns and cities, face the highest risk due to high population densities (more people likely to be impacted). Urbanisation is rapidly increasing in LIC and NEE cities.

Climate change

Changes in global climate will impact the magnitude and frequency of climatic hazards, such as droughts, wildfires, and tropical storms.

Land use

Changes to the natural environment, such as urbanisation and deforestation, can increase hazard risk for climatic hazards such as flooding.

1. State **two** reasons why the risk of natural hazards is likely to increase in the future. [2]
2. Outline reasons why low income countries (LICs) are more vulnerable to natural hazards. [2]

   1. *Natural hazards are likely to pose a greater risk in the future due to the increase in global population[1] and the increase in extreme weather events, such as intense storms due to increased global temperatures[1].*

   2. *Lower income countries have a lower capacity to cope because they cannot afford well built houses that will resist events such as earthquakes[1] or to educate their population on how to best prepare their families and property for natural hazards[1].*

TECTONIC HAZARDS

Earth's surface is constantly moving as a result of the physical processes that lie beneath the surface. These processes lead to tectonic hazards such as earthquakes and volcanic eruptions.

Structure of the Earth

Inner core

The solid centre of the Earth made up of iron and nickel, with temperatures up to 5,500°C.

Outer core

The liquid layer that surrounds the inner core, it is also made of iron and nickel.

Why does oceanic crust subduct underneath continental crust? [3]

Oceanic crust is denser due to the heavier minerals[1] that are part of its composition, such as iron,[1] whereas the continental crust is less dense due to it being more silica rich,[1] which is a lighter mineral.[1]

Mantle

The mantle is the Earth's thickest layer. It can be split into further layers such as the **asthenosphere** (the semi-molten, upper layer of the mantle) and **lithosphere** (the rigid upper mantle and crust).

Plate tectonics theory

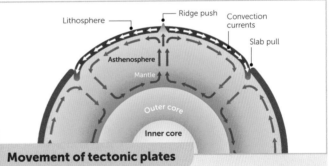

The Earth's crust

Continental crust

- Thicker (30–50km).
- Less dense, doesn't subduct.
- Silica rich rocks.

Oceanic crust

- Thinner (5–10km).
- Very dense, does subduct.
- Iron rich rocks.

Movement of tectonic plates

It is not fully understood how tectonic plates move, but there are two dominant theories. **Convection currents** was the initial theory that was used to explain tectonic movement. It is believed that the heat from the core heats up the semi-liquid mantle and the movement of this magma in a circular motion causes friction to move the tectonic plates along. In recent years a new theory has become more favoured; this is the theory of **slab pull** and **ridge push**. Slab pull is where the weight of the plate being subducted 'pulls' the rest of the plate down. Ridge push is where the new oceanic lithosphere being formed at a mid-ocean ridge 'pushes' the plate along.

PLATE MARGINS

Oceanic and continental plates continuously move and interact with each other at the plate margins.

The global distribution of earthquakes and volcanic eruptions

The locations at which plates meet are referred to as **plate margins**. Different plate margins are associated with different types of hazards. Think about the patterns you can see, and any areas where there are anomalies.

Key

● Earthquake

▲ Volcano

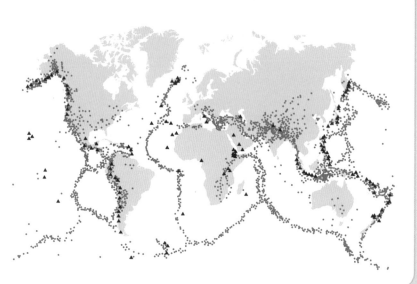

1. Describe the global distribution of tectonic hazards. [2]

2. The diagram shows the plate boundary that runs along the western coast of the USA.

   Using the map (right), explain why San Francisco does not experience volcanic eruptions. [4]

1. *The majority of earthquakes and volcanoes occur in narrow bands along plate margins.[1] However, some volcanoes form in the middle of plates[1] on 'hot spots'. Earthquakes occur across plates, as in North America.[1]*

2. *San Francisco sits on a conservative plate margin[1], where the North American Plate and Pacific Plate move alongside each other.[1] This is shown in the figure as the North American Plate moves in a SE direction and the Pacific Plate moves in a NW direction.[1] No volcanoes occur here as there are no subducting plates to create new magma[1] and no gaps are created between the plates to allow magma through.[1]*

Types of plate margin

There are three types of plate margin: **Destructive**, **Constructive** and **Conservative**.

Destructive	Constructive	Conservative
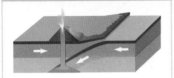		

Destructive

Example:

Peru-Chile trench and the Andes, South America.

Processes

1. Plates move **towards** each other.
2. Dense oceanic plate **subducts** beneath the less dense continental plate. The oceanic plate melts to form viscous, gas-rich **magma**.
3. Plates crumple and lift as they meet, forming fold mountains.

Hazards

Earthquakes – formed due to pressure building and rocks fracturing.

Volcanic eruptions – newly formed magma rises through the crust, erupting violently. Composite volcanoes are formed.

Constructive

Example:

Mid-Atlantic ridge, Atlantic Ocean.

Processes

1. Plates move **away** from each other.
2. As the plates move apart and thin, hot fluid magma rises through cracks between the plates towards the surface, adding new material to the surface. On land, rift valleys form whilst mid-ocean ridges form underwater.

Hazards

Earthquakes – formed due to stretching and fracturing of rock at the plate boundary.

Volcanic eruptions – fast flowing lava erupts gently on the surface, forming shield volcanoes.

Conservative

Example:

San Andreas Fault, USA.

Processes

1. Plates slide past each other.
2. Plates can move in the same direction at different speeds, or can move in opposite directions.

Hazards

Earthquakes – as plates pass each other, friction builds up and plates get locked. Pressure builds until the rocks fracture releasing the built up seismic energy.

There are no volcanic eruptions at this boundary.

You need to study and revise the effects of one tectonic hazard from either earthquakes or volcanoes – this book gives you examples of both on the next pages.

2010 CHILE (HIC)

Named example: Earthquakes

An earthquake is a sudden or violent movement within the Earth's crust followed by a series of shocks. Earthquakes are common across the globe.

The country

- HIC – HDI 0.85 (42nd out of 189 countries).
- GDP per capita: $15,000.

The tectonic setting

Destructive plate boundary – Nazca plate subducts beneath the South American plate.

The earthquake event

- Magnitude 8.8.
- Shallow focus (22 miles / 35 Km).

Effects of a tectonic hazard

Earthquake hazards have both **primary effects** (death, building collapse) and **secondary effects** (disease, landslides) upon the surrounding environment.

Primary effects

- 520 deaths.
- 1.5 million made homeless.
- 220,000 homes damaged.
- Damage estimated to be around $30 billion.
- Santiago airport and Highway 5 (the road running the length of Chile) were badly damaged.

Secondary effects

1500 km of roads damaged by landslides, cutting off communities for days.

Tsunami waves (15m) damaged ports (e.g. Talcahuano), killing 150 and leaving regions without water, light and gas for several days. However many lives were saved due to warning systems.

Responses to a tectonic hazard

The response to an earthquake can have a significant role to play in the overall impacts. **Immediate responses** are as the disaster happens, and in the immediate aftermath (evacuation, search and rescue) with **long-term responses** being in the weeks, months and years after (rebuilding infrastructure).

Immediate responses

- Highway 5 temporarily repaired within a day, allowing aid to be distributed.
- President Bachelet arranged for food retailers to distribute necessities free of charge.
- 10,000 Chilean army troops dispatched to keep the peace and reduce looting.
- 30,000 small emergency shelters funded by a national appeal, whilst 90% of homes had water and power restored in 14 days.

Long-term responses

- 220,000 homes rebuilt by 2014.
- Government was ordered to fund $2.7 million to families of tsunami victims (due to poor information and warnings).

2015 NEPAL (LIC)

Named example: Earthquakes

The country

- LIC – HDI 0.58 (147th out of 189 countries).
- GDP per capita: $905.

The tectonic setting

Destructive plate boundary – Indo-Australian plate colliding with the Eurasian plate.

The earthquake event

- Magnitude 7.8 (and hundreds of aftershocks).
- **Very** shallow focus (5 miles).

Effects of a tectonic hazard

Primary effects

- 9,000 deaths and over 20,000 injured.
- 3.5 million made homeless.
- 600,000 homes destroyed.
- Cost of damage estimated to be around $5 billion.
- Historic UNESCO sites (e.g. Changu Narayan Temple) destroyed, roads were impassable.
- 50% of shops destroyed, impacting food supplies.

Secondary effects

- Landslides wiped out terraced farms and cattle. Re-activated in the summer months due to heavy monsoonal rains.
- Kali Gandaki River blocked by landslides, many people evacuated with fears that flooding may hit.
- Avalanches on Mt. Everest killed 20 people, with 150 more being killed in surrounding valleys.
- Fuel shortages suspended relief operations for months from September.

Responses to a tectonic hazard

Immediate responses

- Most aid brought in by helicopter as many roads were damaged or blocked by slides.
- China and India committed over $1 billion to support Nepal.
- UK sent 100 search and rescue responders, medical experts and disaster experts.
- 500,000 tents erected across Nepal, including 'Tent City' in Kathmandu.

Long-term responses

- New taskforce created to help deal with future earthquakes. A conference was held in 2015 to seek technical and financial support from other countries.
- Earthquake drills now take place across Nepal and people are being educated.
- Stricter controls on building controls to help reduce the impact of future earthquakes.
- 7000 schools rebuilt or repaired.
- Tourism to be boosted – in late 2015 some UNESCO sites opened again and Everest base camp was repaired.

2018 KILAUEA, USA (HIC)

Named example: Volcanoes

The country

USA – HDI 0.926 (17th out of 189 countries), State of Hawaii - HDI 0.945

GDP per capita: $58,181

The tectonic setting

Pacific Plate tectonic hotspot – Intraplate volcanism

The volcanic event

Volcanic explosivity index: 3 (moderate eruption)
Volcano type: Shield volcano/fissure eruptions
Main hazards: Lava flows and volcanic gases

Effects of a tectonic hazard

Volcanic hazards have both **primary** and **secondary effects** upon the surrounding environment.

Primary effects

- Earthquakes caused the volcanic crater to collapse, resulting in an explosive eruption and a large ash plume that reached 30,000 feet (9,144 metres).
- USGS Observatory at the summit of Kilauea was destroyed in the eruption.
- 700 houses and 13 miles of public roads were destroyed due to lava flows.
- 2000 people displaced.
- 24 people injured.

Secondary effects

- New land created along the south east coastline of Hawaii.
- Impacts on tourism in Hawaii due to large areas of the national park being closed off.
- Ban on development in the areas impacted by the eruption.
- Damage cost about $800 million in total.

Responses to a tectonic hazard

The response to a volcanic eruption can have a significant role to play in the overall impacts.

Immediate responses

- Residents impacted by the eruption were evacuated.
- Scientists brought in to monitor the eruption and predict the pathway of flows.
- Temporary repairs to roads impacted by lava flows.
- US Military provided transportation for rapid evacuations.

Long-term responses

- Ban on development in the areas impacted by the eruption.
- National parks opened up again once the eruption was over in early September.
- New USGS summit observatory has been built.
- Improvements to hazard management systems in Hawaii.

2018 FUEGO, GUATEMALA (LIC)

Named example: Volcanoes

The country

Guatemala – HDI 0.651 (127th out of 189 countries)
GDP per capita: $4,478

The tectonic setting

Destructive boundary – Cocos plate being subducted underneath the Caribbean plate.

The volcanic event

Volcanic explosivity index (VEI): 3
Volcano type: Stratovolcano
Main hazards: Pyroclastic flows, lahars (mudflows) and ash plumes.

Effects of a tectonic hazard

Primary effects

- Between 190 and 300 people are believed to have died.
- The village of San Miguel Los Lotes was completely destroyed.
- La Reunion golf course and resort partially destroyed.
- RN-14 road bridge was partially destroyed.
- Coffee, corn and bean crops destroyed.

Secondary effects

- Economic damage due to the road bridge being destroyed as this was a main route linking the city of Antigua to the coast of Guatemala.
- Unemployment due to La Reunion golf course closing down.
- Distrust in local and national governments.

Responses to a tectonic hazard

Immediate responses

- Search and rescue operations started as soon as it was safe to do so, but frequently stopped due to lahars.
- Three days of national mourning.
- Evacuation shelters set up in nearby towns.

Long-term responses

- RN-14 road bridge rebuilt.
- The site of San Miguel Los Lotes was declared a permanent danger zone, meaning no development can occur there.
- Government bodies responsible for hazard management restructured to be better prepared in the future.

Figure 1

Figure 2

Figure 1 Kathmandu, Nepal, January 2016. An aerial view of a refugee camp for people affected by the earthquake in the April of 2015.

Figure 2 Shows volunteers loading supplies in Antigua to take to the area affected by the eruption of Fuego volcano on 3 June 2018.

Using the figures and an example you have studied, suggest why it often takes longer for low income countries (LIC) to recover from tectonic hazards. [6]

Access to technology, Internet and mobile phone usage may be limited within the area pictured in Figure 1. This will lead to a lot of confusion and panic within communities, slowing down evacuation and will make it difficult for disaster managers to quickly identify areas at risk. Aid may also need to come from other countries if the government cannot afford it, which will also take time and extend the recovery process.

Earthquake focus:
Nepal relied on surrounding countries such as India and China for funding (£1 billion), whereas wealthier countries such as Chile were able to quickly restart their main economy (Copper) without any international support. LICs are more likely to have people living in temporary housing and tents such as Tent City in Kathmandu and the makeshift shelters in Figure 1 as they cannot afford to rebuild quickly. Communities can remain cut off for months as roads remain blocked by debris which would likely have been cleared more quickly in wealthier areas.

Volcano focus:
Guatemala relied on both national and international aid to help in its recovery of the eruption at Fuego volcano, whereas the USA didn't require much aid in response to Kilauea, as it is much more developed. Guatemala faced a wide range of social and political impacts, such as distrust of local and national government agencies. The loss of the RN-14 road bridge also significantly impacted the local economy which also meant it has taken the area longer to recover.

Level 3: 6 marks.

This levels-based question should be marked in accordance with the mark bands provided on page 178.

LIVING ON A PLATE MARGIN

Plate margins often run beneath densely populated areas. This map shows population density in relation to global plate boundaries.

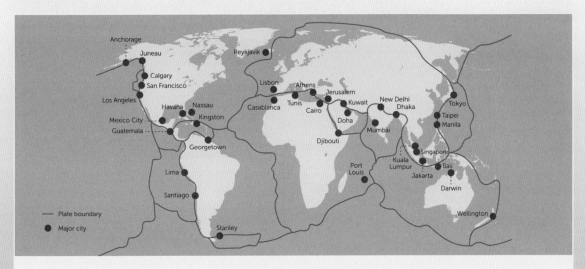

There are many reasons why people live in tectonically active areas:

Poverty

Poverty-stricken areas have more immediate risks to focus on (e.g. food and security).

Desirability

Plate margins often align with desirable areas to live, such as coastal areas.

Water

Water can spring up through fault lines, providing a water supply to arid regions.

Environmental

Volcanic regions offer fertile soils, geothermal energy, minerals and tourism opportunities.

Why do people live in tectonically active areas?

Frequency and awareness

Tectonic events don't happen often. People may also be unaware of the risk.

Technology

Advances in technology and prediction reduce the risks, such as earthquake resistant buildings, tsunami warning systems and volcanic hazard mapping.

Explain **one** economic benefit of living in an area with high hazard risk. [2]

Job opportunities increase[1] through potential tourism,[1] mining[1] and geothermal energy industries.[1] Farming and agriculture may improve[1] with higher quality crops, or higher yields.[1]

REDUCING THE RISK OF TECTONIC HAZARDS

There are many different management strategies used to deal with **either earthquakes or volcanic eruptions**.

Earthquakes

Monitoring

Detecting warning signs.
- Changes in gas (e.g. radon) emissions.
- Smaller 'foreshocks' monitoring changes in ground pressure.
- **Earthquakes occur with very little warning.**

Prediction

Using historical evidence to predict trends.
- Mapping historical events along plate margin. However, these are often inaccurate.

Protection

Designing urban areas to withstand hazards.
- Earthquake-resistant infrastructure (e.g. rubber shock absorbers in deep foundations or cross-bracing).
- Evacuation routes clearly signposted.

Volcanoes

Monitoring

- Satellites can identify:
  - Ground deformation (GPS).
  - Ground heat increasing (infrared).
- Seismometers (rising magma creates earthquakes).

Prediction

- Monitoring (see above) allows accurate prediction of an eruption.

Protection

- Lava and lahar diversion channels.
- Strong, angled rooftops to withstand volcanic ash/debris.
- Evacuation routes clearly signposted.

Planning

Identifying and avoiding places most at risk.
- Hazard mapping and risk assessments to identify high risk areas. In these locations, building can be restricted and immediate evacuation can be prioritised.

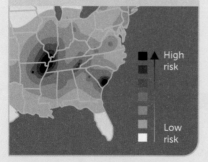

Seismic hazard map, eastern coast of the USA

High risk

Low risk

Explain **two** reasons why HICs often face lower hazard risk than LICs from a tectonic hazard. [4]

HICs can reduce hazard risk because they are able to invest in high quality planning, protection and monitoring systems.[1] These could be systems such as earthquake resistant buildings[1] which have been built or retrofitted to withstand the power of an earthquake using techniques such as cross-bracing.[1] This was shown in Chile (2010) where, owing to a better prepared and more risk aware population,[1] the impacts were significantly less than those seen in Nepal (2015).[1]

WEATHER HAZARDS

Weather hazards exist in many forms across the world. To understand the distribution and patterns of these hazards, it is important to understand how the air within the atmosphere circulates on a global scale.

Global atmospheric circulation

Hadley cells

This atmospheric cell is found between the Equator and the tropics (0°–30° latitude). Hot, moist air rises at the Equator. This is due to the highest concentration of solar energy (intense insolation).

Ferrel cells

This atmospheric cell is found between the tropics and the polar region (30° - 60°). This cell is driven by convection of the Hadley cell and the Polar cell. The air coming from the tropics is warm and moist.

Polar cells

This atmospheric cell is found in the polar region (60° - 90°), and it is driven by cold dry air descending at the poles.

Hadley, Ferrel and Polar cells occur in both hemispheres.

How global atmospheric circulation affects weather

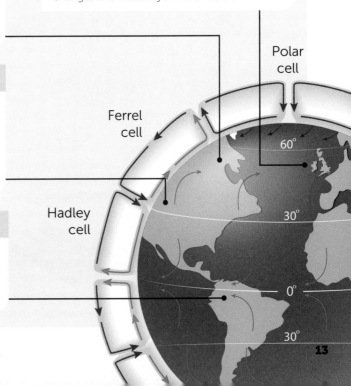

Weather in the UK

The UK experiences lots of cloud and rain formation as it is at 60° north; the point at which the **Ferrel cell** (warm, moist air) and **polar cell** (cold, dry air) meet as **surface winds**. This causes lots of frontal rainfall, pressure changes and instability in the air above us.

Surface winds

These winds form as air moves from areas of high pressure to low pressure to balance out the pressure gradient. There are two main types of surface winds, **trade winds** (found from 30° N and S to the Equator), and the **Westerlies** (found from 30° N and S to the poles).

Deserts

Most deserts occur at 30° north and south on a **high-pressure belt**, where air from both the **Hadley** (equatorial) and **Ferrel** (subtropical) cells is sinking. Clouds cannot form as this warm dry air descends to the ground, creating high daytime temperatures with very little rain.

Rainforests

Rainforests sit on a **low-pressure belt**, as the hot, moist air at the Equator is rising. This rising air quickly cools and condenses whilst still at the Equator, causing intense rainfall.

Polar cell

Ferrel cell

Hadley cell

60°

30°

0°

30°

TROPICAL STORMS

A tropical storm is a huge storm created by intense low pressure. These storms spiral around a calm centre and can bring powerful hurricane force winds (of at least 75 mph) and heavy rain.

Global distribution of tropical storms

Tropical storms are called **hurricanes**, **typhoons** or **cyclones** depending upon which ocean they form. They form only in the tropics (5–30° N/S of the Equator) where they have the right conditions during later summer and early autumn.

Areas prone to tropical storms ●

Give **two** reasons for the distribution of tropical storms as shown in the map above. [2]

Tropical storms only occur in tropical oceans where sea surface temperatures regularly exceed 27°C.[1] These areas are also hot and humid,[1] which promotes cloud formation. The Coriolis Effect is strong enough in the tropics to create a spinning effect on the storm.[1]

The structure of a tropical storm

Tropical storms are very large systems, and can be up to 300 miles across. The shape of a tropical storm is roughly symmetrical. The centre of the storm is called the **eye**. Here, cool, dry air descends leading to dry and calm conditions. The eye wall, which borders the eye of the storm is the most violent part of the storm, with the highest wind speeds, due to the intense pressure differences between the wall and the eye. Beyond the eye wall there are repeated bands of thunderstorms, which get gradually weaker the further from the eye.

Warm air rises
Cold air falls
Eye wall
Rain bands
Eye
Direction of storm rotation

How tropical storms are measured

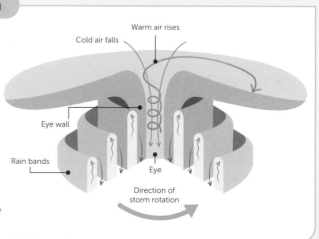

Tropical storms are measured using the **Saffir-Simpson scale**.

1	119–153 kph 74–95 mph	2	154–177 kph 96–110 mph	3	178–208 kph 111–129 mph	4	209–251 kph 130–156 mph	5	>252 kph >157 mph
	Minimal Damage		Moderate Damage		Extensive Damage		Extreme Damage		Catastrophic Damage

Formation of tropical storms

1

A strong upward movement of air draws water vapour up from the warm ocean surface. The water vapour condenses and this forms large cumulonimbus clouds (thunderstorms).

2

Rising air creates a low-pressure area at the ocean surface. Strong winds form as air rushes in to balance out the pressure gradient.

3

As water vapour condenses within the rising air, **latent heat** is released.

4

The cumulonimbus clouds (thunderclouds) combine to create a column of clouds, which spin due to the **Coriolis Effect**.

5

The trade winds move the storm system in a westerly direction.

6

In the centre of the storm, the '**eye**' forms, as cold, dense air rapidly sinks. This region is clear, dry and calm.

7

The storm will continue to pick up in size and strength as it moves across the ocean with the prevailing wind. This is because new 'fuel' in water vapour and latent heat energy are picked up from the water.

8

As it hits the coast, or moves into cooler waters, the tropical storm loses energy as its source of heat and moisture (the ocean) is lost. The storm will gradually slow and weaken over land. It also loses speed over land due to contact with the rough terrain.

Climate change

Climate change is having an impact on the **intensity**, **frequency** and **distribution** of tropical storm events. This is related to the warming of oceans which can increase the amount of water that is evaporated and increase the release of latent heat, making storms more intense. Oceans can also stay warmer for longer, increasing the length of time when tropical storms can form and potentially increasing frequency. Oceans of a more northern and southern latitude could become warm enough for tropical storms to form, increasing their distribution.

2013 THE PHILIPPINES (LIC)

Named example: Typhoon Haiyan

The country	Causes	The tropical storm event
LIC – HDI 0.691 (111 out of 189 countries) GDP per capita: $2,871	Formed in the Pacific Ocean at 13°N in ocean temperatures over 27.5 °C.	Category 5 storm, wind speeds of up to 196 mph, heavy rainfall up to 400 mm in places and a 7 m storm surge.

Effects of a tropical storm

Primary effects

- 6,300 deaths (mostly due to coastal flooding from the storm surge).
- 600,000 people displaced and over 40,000 homes damaged or destroyed.
- 30,000 fishing boats destroyed.
- Major damage to Tacloban Airport.

Secondary effects

- 6,000,000 people lost their main source of income.
- Landslides blocked roads and impacted the response efforts.
- Looting and violence in Tacloban.
- Shortages of basic resources, such as food, water and energy. This led to small outbreaks of disease.

Responses to a tropical storm

Immediate responses

- Evacuation of over 750,000 residents in the days before the typhoon hit.
- Field hospitals set up to reduce pressure on health services.
- Philippines Red Cross delivered food supplies.
- International governments and aid agencies responded quickly with food aid, water and shelters.

Long-term responses

- Rebuilding of roads, bridges and airport facilities.
- Oxfam replaced fishing boats as they are a key source of income in the area.
- 'Cash for work' programmes helped people rebuild.
- Land use planning, new houses built away from areas at high risk of flooding.
- No build zone along the coast in Eastern Visayas, meaning no new developments can be created in these areas.

1. Study the map showing the track of Typhoon Haiyan in November 2013. Describe the track of Typhoon Haiyan between Tuesday 5th November and Sunday 10th November 2013. [2]

Map showing the track of Typhoon Haiyan as it passed over the Philippines.

Before Tuesday at 6am, the typhoon was moving in a westerly direction.[1] At this point, it shifted direction slightly to the north west and headed for the Philippines,[1] hitting the centre of the island nation on Friday at 6am. The eye of the storm passed to the south of Manila[1] before continuing in the same direction towards Vietnam,[1] where it made landfall on Sunday 10th.

Destroyed homes after Hurricane Sandy in the flooded neighbourhood of Breezy Point in the Far Rockaway area, New York City, NY on 12th November, 2012.

2. Using the image above and a named example you have studied, assess the economic and social impacts of tropical storms. [9]

Social impacts left behind by a tropical storm have an effect on people and communities. People may die because of flooding due to storm surges. Homes may also have been damaged or destroyed due to storm surges or high wind speeds. This will have an impact on the local community's quality of living. Typhoon Haiyan, 2013, saw upwards of 6,300 deaths and many more injured. Power cuts can also be caused as electricity cables are damaged in high winds. The figure above shows a large about of damage to the Breezy Point neighbourhood in New York City, this will have social impacts as some people may have been killed or injured in the tropical storm, causing an immediate impact to their families.

The damage to infrastructure such as roads and bridges may also have had an impact on the economy of the areas affected by tropical storms. In the Tacloban area of the Philippines, there was a major impact to the local economy because a large number of fishing boats were destroyed and that is one of the largest industries in this area of the Philippines, leading to increase rates of unemployment. Hurricane Sandy could have caused significant damage to the economy. The damage shown in the figure suggests that a large area of land was damaged, and this will likely have had an impact on the local economy as businesses will have had to close, leading to an increase in unemployment in the affected areas.

Overall, tropical storms have significant primary impacts with a mixture of both social impacts which affect people, and economic impacts that affects money and jobs.

Max level 2 for not using the figure above or a named example you have studied. This levels-based question should be marked in accordance with the mark bands provided on page 178.

REDUCING THE EFFECTS OF TROPICAL STORMS

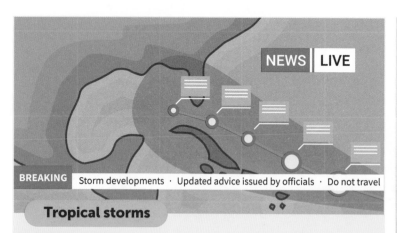

NEWS | LIVE

BREAKING   Storm developments · Updated advice issued by officials · Do not travel

Tropical storms

Monitoring

Detecting warning signs.

- Due to advances in technology, such as weather satellite systems, the ability to monitor the conditions in a tropical storm has improved. This can help alert a government agency to the threat of a potential tropical storm.

Prediction

Using historical evidence to predict trends.

- Using weather systems, meteorologists can predict the approximate direction of the tropical storm, however, the greater the distance from the storm, the more likely the prediction could be inaccurate.

Protection

Designing urban areas to withstand hazards.

- Reinforce buildings to withstand the high winds.
- Storm drains built to remove excessive rainfall and prevent flooding.
- Sea walls to protect settlements from storm surges.

Planning

Identifying and avoiding places most at risk.

- Land use planning involving identifying the areas at highest risk of different hazards, and implementing rules to specify what the land can be used for.

Government multi-purpose cyclone shelters at the coastal village of Bara Arjyapalli of Ganjam district, Odisha, India.

Suggest **two** ways the cyclone shelter in the photograph could be a safe place to evacuate to during a tropical storm. [2]

The cyclone shelter shown in the figure has been built on stilts which effectively reduces the risk of a storm surge flooding the shelter as the water can pass beneath.[1] The building has been built using concrete which is a strong material likely to withstand the high winds of a tropical storm.[1] There may be many drains around the shelter to remove excess rainfall and prevent flooding in the building.[1] Wooden shutters are used which reduce the risk of injury from broken glass and can withstand extreme winds.[1]

UK WEATHER HAZARDS

Extreme weather is very severe, unusual or out of season. This type of weather can also bring about dangers to people, property and infrastructure.

Why does extreme weather happen in the UK?

UK weather can be impacted due to the multiple air masses that can dominate; each different air mass brings a different type of weather.

Anticyclones	Depressions
Anticyclones are high air pressure systems. Descending air prevents clouds from forming. In summer, this brings warm, dry weather, and in winter, it will bring cold, dry weather.	**Depressions** are low air pressure systems where air is rising. As the air rises, clouds form as water vapour which condenses, bringing wet, windy and unsettled weather.

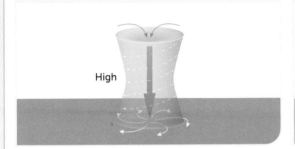

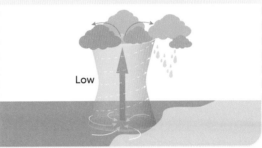

What are the UK's weather hazards?

Thunderstorms

Thunderstorms can bring lightning, rain, thunder and hail which can damage property and cause injuries.

Rain

Rain can cause flooding, which can have social, economic and environmental impacts on the local area.

Drought and heat waves

Long periods of hot weather can cause humans and animals to suffer from heat exhaustion, and will deplete water supplies in parts of the UK.

Snow and ice

This weather phenomenon can bring large scale disruption to transport infrastructure. The most vulnerable may also suffer from colder temperatures.

Wind

Strong winds can cause destruction and disruption to infrastructure.

Which **one** of the following is an example of extreme weather?

A. A wet spring in Wales

B. A sunny July in SE England

C. Storm Eunice hits England

D. A frosty morning in January

[1]

Answer: C.[1]

IS UK WEATHER GETTING MORE EXTREME?

Heavy rainfall and flooding

There is evidence that the UK climate is getting wetter. There has been a 4% increase in rainfall totals over the decade 2008–2017 compared with those from 1961–1990. There has also been a 17% increase in extremely wet days in the same time period. Climate scientists have said that risk of flooding in the UK has increased by at least 20%, and that wet winters such as those seen in 2013/14 and 2015/16 are seven times more likely than 1961–1990.

Heatwaves

There is evidence that the UK is not only getting warmer but the length of hot spells is also increasing. In the decade 2008–2017 there was a 0.8°C increase in the temperatures of the hottest days of the year, and the length of warm spells had doubled from 5.3 days to just over 13 days in the same time period. It is likely that the record breaking summer temperatures of 2018 are 30 times more likely to happen now than in 2008.

Drought

Overall, there has been a decline in the length of dry spells in the UK. However long dry spells are not the official definition of droughts which require a combination of meteorological, hydrological and societal factors to combine to cause them. It is likely that summers will be drier in the future and this could have knock-on impacts, e.g. water rationing, wildfires and crop failure.

Cold events

Evidence shows that there are fewer days of frost in the decade 2008–2017 than the period of 1961–1990. This is what is expected with a warming climate which is going to see wetter and warmer winters, and warmer and drier summers in the UK. However, cold snap events are likely to be more extreme, such as in December 2010, which was the coldest December in 100 years.

Wind storms

There is limited evidence to suggest that wind events are going to get worse, and that the record number of storms over the British Isles in the winter of 2013/14 couldn't be linked to human-induced climate change.

The graph opposite shows the frequency of heavy rainfall events in each year. A 1 in 100 average indicates one heavy rainfall event over 100 days. Over time, this gives a view of the frequency of 'extreme' rainfall.

Analyse the graph and describe what it shows about the frequency of heavy rainfall events each year in the UK. [2]

The graph suggests that heavy rainfall events are becoming more common over the period of time shown.[1] You can see that the five year running mean has increased from about 1 in 120 days in 1962, to 1 in 95 days in 2010.[1]

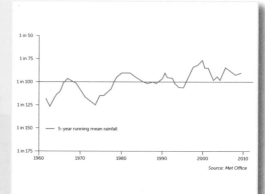

Source: Met Office

2014 SOMERSET LEVELS FLOODING

Extreme weather event in the UK

Causes

- 350mm of rain in January and February due to a series of south westerly depressions.
- High tides and storm surges in the Bristol Channel.
- Rivers hadn't been dredged for 20 years which led to significant sediment build-up in lots of rivers, including the River Parrett.

Social impacts

- Over 600 houses flooded, and entire villages cut off, disrupting businesses, schools and livelihoods.

Economic impacts

- Damage cost was in the order of £147 million.
- Impacts on farming businesses in the local area: over 1,000 livestock were evacuated, and 14,000 ha of farmland were flooded.
- Infrastructure was damaged, such as power supplies, roads and railways.

Environmental impacts

- Flood water was polluted with sewage and oil.
- Large amounts of debris left behind from the floods which needed clearing.

Responses

Immediate responses

- Villages such as Moorland were evacuated.
- People used boats to travel.
- The floods gained a large amount of media interest.

Long-term responses

- £20 million Flood Action Plan launched, created by Somerset County Council and the Environment Agency.
- 8km of Rivers Tone and Parrett dredged.
- Infrastructure in the area was adapted to manage the flood risk, such as roads being raised to reduce impacts of flooding.
- Possible tidal barrage to be built in Bridgwater Bay to help reduce tidal flood risk.

Dredging the river to increase water capacity

EVIDENCE FOR CLIMATE CHANGE

Longer term evidence for climate change

Tree rings

Each year a tree grows (dependent on the climate) tree rings are created. The width of the rings can be used to show when a year has been warmer (more growth) or cooler (less growth). This can be used to get a generic idea of how the Earth's climate has changed year on year.

Ice cores

When ice forms, small concentrations of atmospheric gases are trapped. These can be used to reveal the composition of the atmosphere at that point in time, and an average temperature can then be worked out. Ice core data can go back up to 800,000 years. This has been used to show natural variations in the Earth's climate over time, with a rapid increase in recent years.

Sediment layers

Similar to ice cores, gases trapped in ocean sediments, as well as mineral and chemical composition can be used to show the makeup of the atmosphere at time of deposition. This can help reconstruct Earth's climate over time.

Recent evidence

Rising ocean levels

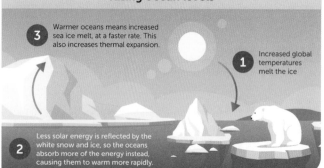

3 — Warmer oceans means increased sea ice melt, at a faster rate. This also increases thermal expansion.

1 — Increased global temperatures melt the ice

2 — Less solar energy is reflected by the white snow and ice, so the oceans absorb more of the energy instead, causing them to warm more rapidly.

Shrinking glaciers and melting sea ice

There is photographic evidence that shows that glaciers are in retreat all over the world. This is caused when the rate of ice melting is quicker than the rate of ice accumulation. They are decreasing due to changes in climate and increasing global temperatures decreasing the level of snowfall in many areas.

Thermometer readings

Since records began, there has been a steady increase in the average global temperature recorded and the average air temperature has increased by around 1°C since records began in 1900. However, over the last decade, we have seen an increasing number of years classified as the 'hottest recorded'.

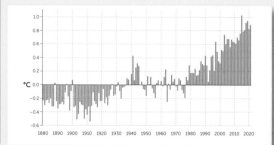

Describe the trend of the average global surface temperature on the graph. [2]

The trend is showing that global surface temperatures are increasing.[1] This can be seen from the 1990s onwards where most years are above the average temperature.[1]

Award one mark for describing the trend, and a 2nd mark for using data from the graph to support it.

CAUSES OF CLIMATE CHANGE

Natural causes of climate change

Orbital variations | Milankovitch Cycles

Changes in the Earth's distance to the sun has an impact on whether the Earth is going through a period of warming or cooling.

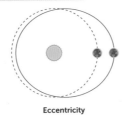

Eccentricity

24.5° 21.5°

Obliquity (Tilt)

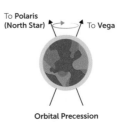

To Polaris (North Star) — To Vega

Orbital Precession

Eccentricity

Every 100,000 years, Earth's orbit goes from being almost circular, to more elliptical. The more elliptical, the more solar energy that reaches the Earth, causing warming.

Axial tilt

Every 41,000 years, the Earth's axis tilts from 21.5° to 24.5°. The steeper the tilt, the more extreme the seasons are as more solar energy reaches the hemispheres in summer.

Precession

Every 26,000 years the Earth's axis wobbles (like a spinning top toy). This can cause greater seasonal extremes for the different hemispheres.

Solar output

The sun goes through an approximate 11-year cycle where sunspot activity (dark patches with reduced surface temperature), and solar flares (increased surface temperatures) change. This has an impact on the solar heat energy reaching Earth, and therefore impacts Earth's climate.

Volcanic activity

Volcanic ash and certain volcanic gases can block out/reflect solar energy from reaching the Earth's surface. This will therefore have a short term cooling effect on the planet.

Human causes of climate change

Greenhouse effect vs Enhanced greenhouse effect.

The greenhouse effect is naturally occurring as gases such as carbon dioxide and methane keep the Earth naturally insulated at a liveable temperature. With the human enhanced greenhouse effect, we are seeing human activities causing an increase in the concentration of these greenhouse gases.

- Burning of fossil fuels as an energy source releases CO_2.
- Deforestation removes an important carbon sink allowing more CO_2 in the atmosphere.
- Increased agriculture such as livestock and rice farming releases more methane. Farming is needed to provide food to increasing populations around the globe.

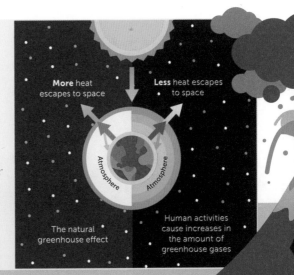

More heat escapes to space

Less heat escapes to space

Atmosphere

Atmosphere

The natural greenhouse effect

Human activities cause increases in the amount of greenhouse gases

MANAGING CLIMATE CHANGE – MITIGATION

Mitigation strategies are about reducing or preventing the effects of climate change.

Alternative energy sources

Burning fossil fuels is one of the main causes of human enhanced climate change. Using alternative energy sources, such as solar power, hydro-electric power (HEP), wind power and nuclear power helps reduce the amount of carbon dioxide being released into the atmosphere.

In the UK in 2020, 43.1% of power generation was from renewable energy sources, with 24% of this being from wind energy.

International agreements

There have been several international agreements which are aimed at reducing the rate of climate change, these include the Kyoto Protocol and the Paris Agreement. Every year the UN holds a conference called the Conference of the Parties (COP) to assess the progress being made in dealing with climate change. It has been held since 1995, and aims to get every nation to reach an agreement on how to address climate change.

Carbon capture and storage technology

This technology will remove the carbon dioxide from industrial processes and power generation and prevent it from entering the atmosphere. This will therefore reduce the amount of carbon dioxide being released into the atmosphere. The carbon dioxide is then compressed and stored deep underground, often in old oil and gas reservoirs. This technology is still extremely expensive and will not necessarily be viable in many economies.

CO_2

Planting trees

Trees act as natural carbon sinks because they take in carbon dioxide during photosynthesis. The process of planting trees is called afforestation.

In November 2021, COP26 was held in Glasgow. By the end of the conference, a non-legally binding agreement to stop and reverse deforestation was signed by over 100 nations, including Brazil.

Give **one** advantage and **one** disadvantage of international agreements as a mitigation strategy for climate change. [2]

Advantages: Global consensus against climate change,[1] frequent reviews of policies to make sure they are working and effective.[1]

Disadvantages: Countries are not legally bound to stick to agreements,[1] countries can leave the agreements.[1]

MANAGING CLIMATE CHANGE – ADAPTATION

Adaptation strategies do not aim to prevent climate change. Instead they aim to limit the impacts caused by a changing climate.

Longer term evidence for climate change

Adapting to rising sea levels

With sea levels rising more than 20 cm since the 1880s, low lying places are becoming more vulnerable to coastal flooding, extreme weather events and coastal erosion. Countries such as Bangladesh and the Maldives would fall largely underwater. There are many different strategies to adapting to these conditions (see **page 60** for more detail):

Hard engineering coastal defences/flood defences

Building physical structures to reduce the risk of flooding in an area. Examples include sea walls.

Soft engineering strategies such as wetland

The natural environment is developed to reduce flood risk e.g. creating wetlands which act as a natural flood defence.

Land use planning

Only allowing certain structures to be built in flood prone areas, or changing structures so they are on higher foundations to reduce risk from flooding (this is seen in many places already such as the Maldives).

Managed retreat and evacuation

People and infrastructure are moved away from areas that are at risk of flooding. Low lying countries such as the Maldives have considered buying land from other countries and moving their population before the islands become uninhabitable.

Agriculture adaptations

Farmers need to adapt to climate change as certain crops are unable to grow in a changing climate. This can be done by using genetically altered crops, such as those more resistant to drought. Changing cropping patterns can be used to suit the new climatic conditions; as climates become warmer, fruits and vegetables that would previously be grown in tropical climates can be produced elsewhere.

Water supply adaptations

Water transfer schemes can be used to move water from areas of water surplus to areas of water deficit. Schemes such as rainwater harvesting can also increase the infrastructure surrounding local schemes.

Give **one** advantage and **one** disadvantage of hard engineering as an adaptation strategy for climate change. [2]

Advantages: It is very effective from preventing flooding.[1] It can protect large settlements for longer meaning that long term plans can be made.[1]

Disadvantages: It is expensive to build.[1] It is not a permanent solution and will need maintenance and upgrading.[1]

EXAMINATION PRACTICE

1. After a hazardous event, responses are made.

    State **one** difference between primary responses and secondary responses. [1]

2. Which **one** of the following statements is a condition required for a tropical storm to form? [1]

    A. ☐ Warm dry air

    B. ☐ Ocean temperatures below 20°C

    C. ☐ A location 30° north or south of the Equator

    D. ☐ Warm moist air

3. Complete the following paragraph to explain how latent heat contributes to the formation of a tropical storm.

    Latent heat is the energy released when water changes _____ in processes such as condensation. This additional energy adds fuel to the storm, creating strong _____ and increasing the speed of _____ rising within the storm.

You are required to study one tectonic hazard from either earthquakes or volcanoes. Your answers to related questions can refer to either.

Note: A 9-mark question in this section will have 3 additional marks for spelling, punctuation, grammar (SPaG) and your use of specialist terminology.

4. State **one** tectonic hazard that can occur at a conservative plate boundary. [1]

5. 'Primary effects of tectonic hazards are more destructive than secondary effects.'

    To what extent do you agree with this statement?

    Use your own knowledge as well as an example you have studied. [9]

6. State what is meant by 'extreme weather'. [1]

7. Name an example of an extreme weather event in the UK. [1]

8. Explain why the UK experiences many different types of weather. [2]

9. Explain **two** ways in which weather in the UK is becoming more extreme. [4]

10. Explain how extreme weather can have social and environmental impacts. Use a named example to support your answer. [6]

11. Describe **one** natural cause of climate change. [2]

12. State **one** difference between the natural greenhouse effect and the enhanced greenhouse effect. [2]

13. Give **two** types of evidence for climate change. [2]

14. Describe the difference between mitigation and adaptation. [1]

15. Suggest **two** ways to mitigate against climate change. [4]

16. **Figure 1** shows a plate boundary.

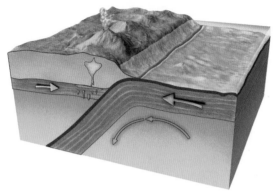

Figure 1

   (a)   Name the plate boundary. [1]

   (b)   If the boundary in Figure 1 is moving at a rate of 2.5 cm per year, calculate how far it would move in 250 years. Answers to the nearest metre. [1]

       A. ☐ 6 m

       B. ☐ 63 m

       C. ☐ 100 m

       D. ☐ 625 m

17. Name the most destructive area of a tropical storm. [1]

18. Explain why tropical storms do not form on the Equator. [2]

19. 'As earthquake magnitude increases, so does the number of associated deaths.'

    Do you agree? Use evidence from the table of data below to support your answer [2]

Year and location	Magnitude	Fatalities
Indian Ocean earthquake and tsunami, 2004	9.1	227,898
Haiti earthquake, 2010	7.0	160,000
Sichuan earthquake, 2008	7.9	87,587
Kashmir earthquake, 2005	7.6	87,351
Bam (Iran) earthquake, 2003	6.6	26,271
Tohoku earthquake and tsunami, 2011	9.0	20,896

20. Explain how surface winds form. [2]

ECOSYSTEMS

Ecosystems are communities of organisms and the environment in which they interact.

Interrelationships within a small scale ecosystem

- **Biotic** – living i.e. plants and animals
- **Abiotic** – non-living i.e. soils and water

Food web

An example of a small scale UK ecosystem is a **temperate deciduous woodland**.

The arrows show how energy flows through the woodland ecosystem. In a **food chain** one flow of energy is shown, but in a **food web** you can see multiple flows. The food web shows:

- **Producers** – gain their energy from the sun.
- **Primary consumers** – gain their energy by eating producers.
- **Secondary consumers** – gain their energy by eating primary consumers.

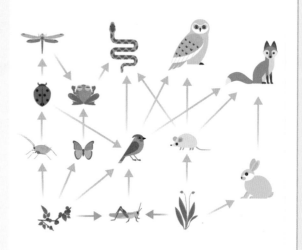

Nutrient cycle

The woodland **nutrient cycle** shows how the living organisms (biotic components or biomass) fall to the floor when they die and are broken down by **decomposers** e.g. bacteria, fungi or insects.

The nutrients become part of the soil and are available to be taken up by the plants in the woodland, completing the cycle.

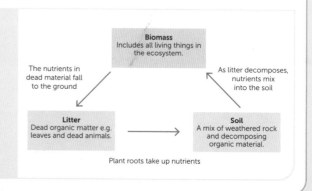

Biomass
Includes all living things in the ecosystem.

The nutrients in dead material fall to the ground

As litter decomposes, nutrients mix into the soil

Litter
Dead organic matter e.g. leaves and dead animals.

Soil
A mix of weathered rock and decomposing organic material.

Plant roots take up nutrients

The balance between components in an ecosystem

Components in an ecosystem need to stay balanced, so if a change happens somewhere in the ecosystem the whole ecosystem must adapt.

Examples

- If foxes in the woodland were hunted, the population of squirrels would increase.
- If trees in the woodland were cut down, there would be less organic matter being decomposed and the soil would start to lose its supply of nutrients.

Large scale natural global ecosystems

Large scale natural global ecosystems are sometimes known as **biomes**. Their distribution and characteristics are given below:

Desert

Dry (arid) conditions along the Tropics mean plants and animals have adapted to survive e.g. cacti and camels.

Taiga

Cool climate with coniferous forests.

Temperate deciduous forest

Mild, wet climate with trees that lose their leaves in winter.

Tropical rainforest

Hot, wet (humid) climate along the Equator means this biome has great biodiversity.

Tundra

Covered in ice, so few plants and animals are found there.

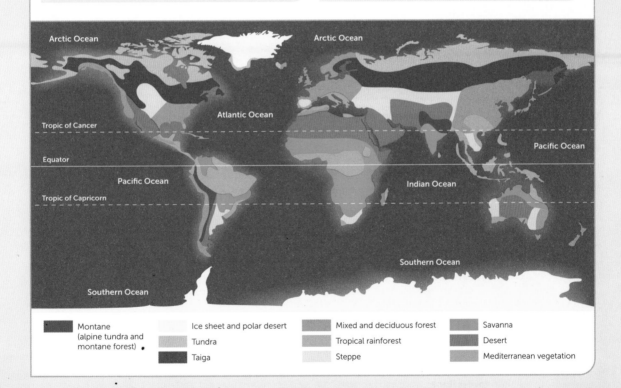

Describe the distribution of the tropical rainforest global ecosystem using the map above. [3]

Tropical rainforests are found along the Equator,[1] with a large area being found in South America.[1] There are no tropical rainforests in Europe.[1]

TROPICAL RAINFOREST CHARACTERISTICS

Tropical rainforests (TRF) are hot all year around as there is intense insolation (heating from the sun) at the Equator. They are wet because of the band of low pressure at the Equator giving heavy daily rainfall.

Rainforest layers

Rainforest layers provide a habitat for different plants and animals that have **adapted** to live there.

Emergent layer   50–80m

The tallest trees form the **emergent layer**, where conditions are hot, wet and windy and so less hospitable for animals. These tall trees have massive **buttress roots** which spread out across the forest floor to keep them stable and to make the most of the nutrients in the top layer of the soil.

Canopy layer   30–50m

The **canopy** is where the branches and leaves of most trees are found and is the layer with the greatest **biodiversity** as it has most sunlight. Epiphytes grow on the branches of trees so they can reach the sunlight and lianas (vines) climb the trees, making it easier for animals such as monkeys and sloths to move around. Huge numbers of insects live in this layer, including many butterflies.

Understorey layer   1–30m

The **understorey layer** includes bushes, vines and small trees with large leaves to maximise energy collected from the sun for photosynthesis as the canopy blocks most sunlight. Snakes such as boa constrictors are found here.

Forest floor

The **forest floor** is dark and humid. The largest animals in the rainforest, such a tapirs, are found here, along with a large number of decomposers such as leaf cutter ants.

The **indigenous people** of the rainforest make their homes on the forest floor and use resources from the forest to meet their needs. Different groups have different lifestyles; some are hunters and gatherers; others use slash and burn to clear land for farming whilst some rely on fishing in the many rivers. Indigenous cultures maintain balance in the ecosystem by using resources **sustainably**.

Climate graph

Revisit your work on the global atmospheric circulation system on page 13.

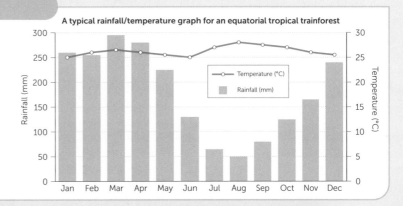

A typical rainfall/temperature graph for an equatorial tropical trainforest

Interdependence of climate, water, soils, plants, animals and people

Water is rapidly cycled in tropical rainforests (**TRF**) as it is so hot. Most rain is **intercepted** by vegetation and then evaporates from its leaves through **evapotranspiration**. Rain reaching the forest floor will **infiltrate**, some will be used by vegetation through its roots and some will become part of the **groundwater** store which feeds into the many rivers found in TRF.

Rainforest soils (**latosols**) are deep due to the supply of **litter** (dead organic matter) and rapid decomposition because of the humidity. Water infiltrating **leaches** the nutrients from the soil, leaving it infertile, except for in the top layer where the litter is being broken down.

Study the photographs below.

(a) Look at **Figure A**. How does the dung beetle shown contribute to the nutrient cycle in the TRF? [2]

(b) Look at **Figures B** and **C**. How have plants adapted to use the sunlight? [4]

Figure A

Figure C

Figure B

(a) *The dung beetle is a decomposer.[1] It breaks down litter and mixes it into the soil.[1]*

(b) *Buttress roots keep trees stable as they grow tall to reach the sunlight. Plants on the forest floor have large dark green leaves to maximise photosynthesis. Lianas climb trees to reach the sunlight. Level 2 – Clear: 4 marks.*

This question should be marked in accordance with the levels-based mark scheme on page 178.

RAINFOREST ANIMAL ADAPTATIONS

Plants and animals of the rainforest

Boa constrictors

Boa constrictors use **camouflage** to blend into the landscape, living on the forest floor and in the understorey. Their muscular bodies allow them to climb trees and also to wrap themselves around their prey until it suffocates. They don't need to move fast as they lie in wait for their prey, often hiding in hollow logs. They eat birds, monkeys, rodents, lizards and bats.

Squirrel monkey

Squirrel monkeys are found in the lower canopy. They use their tails for balance and can move rapidly through the branches, eating insects and fruit. They urinate on their hands and rub this on their feet so they are cooled as the urine evaporates!

This photograph also shows **drip tips** on the end of shiny leaves in the rainforest. This helps the water run off so the leaves don't rot.

Red-eyed tree frog

Red-eyed tree frog eggs are laid on leaves above ponds. When the tadpoles hatch, they fall into the pond, where they feed on tiny insects until they become froglets. They climb up trees near the pond to become tree frogs.

The frogs have green bodies to blend in with the leaves when their eyes are shut and their legs tucked under them, but if a predator strikes, they reveal their red eyes and bright legs to confuse them.

Hyacinth macaw

This hyacinth macaw is the largest flying parrot and lives in hollows in trees or cliffs. It has a strong beak to eat nuts from different species of palms and can even break a coconut if it needs to.

Blue Morpho butterfly

This Blue Morpho is one of the largest butterflies in the world. With bright blue colouring on one side of its wings and dull brown on the other side it can either attract attention or blend in with the trees. The brown side also has eye spots to put off predators. It is usually found with its wings closed on the forest floor, but when it is looking for a mate, it flies through all layers of the forest. The Blue Morpho uses a long proboscis (like a straw) to drink sap, the juice of rotting fruits and fluids of decomposing animals.

DEFORESTATION

Deforestation is the removal of forest. This could be to gain from selling the wood, to use the land for farming, mining or settlement or due to forest fires.

Changing rates of deforestation

The figure below shows the **rates of deforestation** between 2001 and 2020, for forests globally. Rates of deforestation have slowed in recent years as there is more awareness of the value of the world's forests. However, the global pattern hides variations between regions.

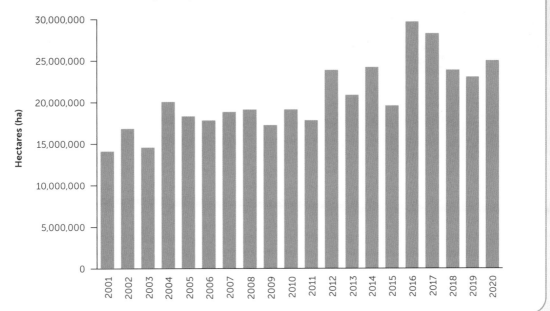

Study the graph above.

(a) Describe the deforestation shown in this graph. [2]

(b) Suggest reasons for the changes in rates of loss of trees from 2001–2020. [3]

(a) *The rate of tree cover loss increases until 2016[1], then the rate of loss decreases until 2020.[1]*

(b) *The rate may have increased as people cut down the trees to sell[1] or to make space for farm land.[1] The rate may have decreased from 2016 if protection measures were put in place.[1]*

CASE STUDY THE AMAZON

Development of rainforests

The Amazon rainforest is the largest in the world and covers parts of eight countries in South America. It is valued for its biodiversity.

Over 30 million people live in the Amazon, including 350 indigenous groups. They value the forest for farming, fishing, traditional medicines and shelter. Rivers such as the Amazon are used for transport.

Rates of deforestation in Brazil were decreasing through conservation efforts and regulation, but a change in leadership saw rates climb from 2019. Rates of deforestation in Peru and Bolivia have increased rapidly in the last decade. These are rapidly developing countries which want to make the most of a valuable resource.

Causes of deforestation

- Developing countries need to improve their **infrastructure** (connections such as roads, Internet and electricity grid).

- **Hydroelectric power** (**HEP**) means more energy for development in countries which are often NEEs. 85% of electricity in Brazil comes from hydropower - the largest dam is the Itaipu Dam.

- There's a high demand for raw materials from the forest, including gold, oil, timber and fish. The Carajas iron ore mine is the largest in the world and employs 3 000 people.

- Growing populations and exports mean more food is needed, with forests cleared to grow crops such as soy and oil palm and to farm cattle for beef.

The Itaipu Dam (Brazil/Paraguay)

Exam tip: When examiners ask you to use an example or a case study, they will expect you to include information specific to the place. Avoid generic answers which could be about anywhere. Learn key facts and figures to add place specific detail to your answers.

Impacts of deforestation

- **Infrastructure** developments such as the Trans-Amazonian Highway can destroy the forest and also open it up to illegal logging.

- **Hydropower** dams block rivers and the reservoirs flood large areas of forest.

- Governments struggle to protect the Amazon from illegal **mining**, **logging** and fishing and mercury pollution from mines is affecting food chains for fish, wildlife and people.

- Clearing forests for farming will affect their ecosystem, but the impact will vary according to the type of farming and the way it is managed. Subsistence farming (small scale farming to meet the needs of a community) has much less of an impact than commercial farming (crops grown for sale to make a profit).

The Amazon Rainforest in South America is the largest in the world

Developments aiming to improve the economy of a country may only lead to a short term gain if the rainforest ecosystem is permanently damaged.

Removing trees means water isn't intercepted and more flows through the soil into the rivers. Nutrients are leached from the soil, leaving it infertile and vulnerable to erosion. The climate becomes drier as there is less evapotranspiration, leading to more forest fires.

Soil erosion near Manaus, Brazil

Explain how development in areas of tropical rainforest harms the environment on a local scale and the global scale.   [6]

Rainforests in the Amazon are burnt to increase land available for grazing cattle. This releases the carbon stored in the wood into the atmosphere in the form of carbon dioxide, which is a greenhouse gas. Greenhouse gases keep heat in the atmosphere and so lead to climate change on a global scale. The Amazon rainforest was a carbon sink, removing carbon dioxide from the atmosphere, but deforestation means this isn't as effective as it used to be.

Deforestation for farming and for mines such as the Carajas iron ore mine also damages the ecosystem at a local scale. Animal habitats are lost and mining can lead to mercury polluting rivers. Soil is washed away as it isn't protected by trees, becoming infertile and barren. As trees aren't retaining water the microclimate will become drier.

This question should be marked in accordance with the levels-based mark scheme on page 178.

SUSTAINABLE MANAGEMENT OF TROPICAL RAINFORESTS

Tropical rainforests are a valuable resource, but are vulnerable to deforestation and exploitation. **Sustainable management** aims to balance the needs of economic development with the protection of the tropical rainforest ecosystem. It means thinking about the needs of people today but also ensuring the rainforest remains healthy for future generations.

Services

The rainforest is a life support system:
- Taking in carbon dioxide from the atmosphere through photosynthesis and storing it as biomass whilst releasing oxygen into the air
- Keeping soils healthy
- Maintaining the water supply through its role in the hydrological cycle

Goods

It also provides a range of goods such as:
- Food e.g. Brazil nuts
- Medicine e.g. quinine to treat malaria
- Cash crops – sold to earn an income e.g. soy
- Raw materials e.g. timber

International agreements

International agreements can make a huge difference to rates of deforestation. The **Amazon Soy Moratorium** stopped companies buying soy from farmers who clear the rainforest. Satellite monitoring means observers see new deforestation and who is doing it. Soy production has increased in Brazil, but very little is grown on newly deforested land.

Selective logging and replanting

Selective logging and replanting means that only damaged or older trees are removed, leaving younger ones to grow. **Education** means that both the producers of rainforest products and the consumers are more aware of the need to **conserve** the rainforest e.g. campaigns to stop deforestation for palm oil. Rainforest conservation has also been boosted by 'debt-for-nature' swaps, where national debts are reduced in exchange for agreements to conserve areas of forest.

Explain how ecotourism can be used to manage rainforest sustainably. [4]

Ecotourism means that rainforest communities can make money by hosting tourists whilst protecting the rainforest for future generations. The Napo Wildlife Center in Ecuador is owned and run by the Kichwa Añangu people who reinvest all earnings in the community. Only 40 people stay there at one time, in lodges made from natural material and with power from solar panels and locally sourced food. This levels-based question should be marked in accordance with the mark bands provided on page 178.

HOT DESERT CHARACTERISTICS

Hot deserts are hot all year around as there is intense insolation (heating from the sun) at the Tropics and few clouds. They are dry because of the band of high pressure at the Tropics.

Climate graph for Riyadh

Students should study and revise either hot deserts or cold environments.

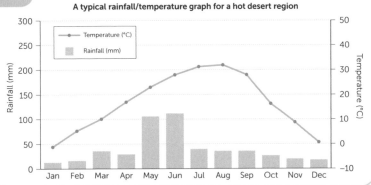

A typical rainfall/temperature graph for a hot desert region

Interdependence of climate, water, soils, plants, animals and people

Desert temperatures are high in the day and cool at night (**diurnal variation**) as there are no clouds. There is little rainfall as this is an area of high pressure and any rain that does fall is quickly evaporated.

Water can be found deep underground and in ephemeral rivers which flow for a short time when rain falls, usually in nearby mountains. When the water table reaches the surface, an oasis may form. Dry conditions mean little vegetation and so poor soil. Desert soils are usually **aridisols**, but if they are really dry they are **entisols**. Deserts may have sand dunes or be gravelly and rocky. Biodiversity is low in the hot desert due to the extreme climate and poor soils.

Indigenous people in the desert are nomadic, moving from place to place to graze their animals. They have great knowledge of where to find water (e.g. oases and boreholes) and how to use the resources of the desert for building, medicine and food. When an animal is killed, every part of it is used. This could be seen as a sustainable way of using the desert as the people live in balance with the environment. Nomadic camps, such as the Bedouin camp in Morocco shown in the photograph, often use woven material for tents, creating areas for people to live as extended families with enclosures for livestock.

Why is biodiversity low in a hot desert? [3]

Hot deserts are very hot and dry which makes it difficult for plants to grow.[1] This means there is little organic matter to enrich the soil[1] and also fewer producers for consumers to eat.[1]

CASE STUDY   THE SAHARA DESERT

Development of hot deserts

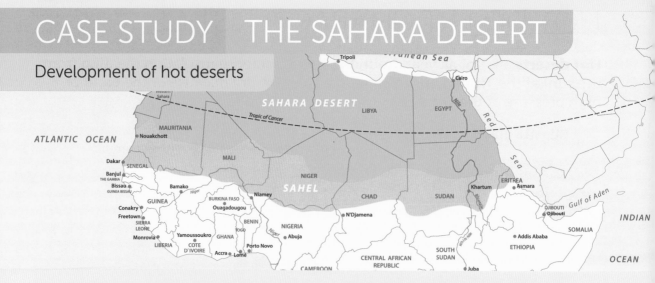

The Sahara is the largest hot desert in the world, covers nearly a third of the continent of Africa and includes parts of 11 countries.

It is dry because it is on the Tropic of Cancer (band of high pressure) but also because it is in the rain shadow of the Atlas Mountains. As well as sand dunes it includes salt flats, plains and depressions. Its two permanent rivers are the Nile and the Niger, but there are also ephemeral rivers, groundwater in aquifers deep below the ground and over 90 oases. Nomadic indigenous people in the Sahara are known as Tuareg and rely on grazing their goats and camels to survive.

Opportunities to develop the desert

Opportunities to develop the desert often combine old and new knowledge and technologies.

- Whilst the Tuareg use traditional methods to graze their herds, new technology such as hydroponics is being used to **farm** in areas previously thought too dry, such as in refugee camps in Algeria.

- Ancient Egypt was famous for its wealth from farming and **mineral extraction**, but modern technology is making the country's gold and iron mines safer and more profitable. An example is Sukari gold mine in the Nubian desert, part of the Sahara.

- The oilfields of Saharan countries such as Algeria are well known, but unsustainable as oil is non-renewable and releases particulates and greenhouse gases when burned. These countries are now seeing growth of renewable **energy sources**, with the 4000 MW Tafouk 1 mega solar scheme being announced in 2020.

- Sahara **tourism** faced setbacks due to terrorist attacks and the COVID 19 pandemic. Visitors to the Sharm el Sheik resort in Egypt can take trips to the Pyramids of Giza or go quad biking in the desert. Mass tourism brings in money, but much is lost through leakage to the big **transnational corporations (TNCs)** which own the hotels, whilst the impact on the fragile desert ecosystem is also a concern. **Ecotourism** is an alternative, using thick stone walls and small windows to keep rooms cool rather than using air conditioning and encouraging tourists to spend money on local goods.

Challenges when developing the desert

Anyone developing the extreme environment of the desert also has **challenges** to overcome

- Temperatures in the Sahara can reach 38°C in the day and drop to −0.5°C a night. This puts stress on roads and bridges as they expand and contract.

- A lack of water makes it hard to develop as farming, mining and tourism all need water. Extracting too much water from aquifers can lead to the ground collapsing and providing water for tourists can mean local people having less. New technology means that water can be carefully recycled, but it is still in short supply.

- The Sahara is immense, with few roads crossing it, making accessibility difficult. In Algeria oil fields have their own airstrips so materials and workers can be flown in and out.

Using a case study, to what extent do challenges outweigh the opportunities for development in a hot desert environment? [9]

Although there are significant challenges in developing the Sahara desert, recent technological developments mean that developers can overcome these challenges to make the most of opportunities in this hot desert environment.

Despite the challenge of transporting machinery, materials and people into remote areas of the desert, the Hassi Messaoud oil field was developed in 1956. Aircraft were used for transport and the small town became the First Energy town in Algeria, housing offices of major oil and gas companies and growing to a population of over 45 000 people. Temperatures reach a maximum of 45°C in July and sand storms are common from March to June, but people have overcome these challenges in order to develop this energy source.

The Tuareg have always kept herds of goats and camels in the Sahara desert, living nomadic lives to make sure their animals have enough to eat. Their simple but carefully considered lifestyle means they can overcome the challenging temperatures and lack of water. The Tuareg wear loose clothes to protect them from the sun and from sandstorms. New techniques such as hydroponics are now being used in dry areas by people such as the Sahrawi refugees in camps in Algeria. A low tech version of hydroponics is used to grow animal feed using 90% less water than usual. The refugees have more milk and meat, improving their food security.

These examples show that opportunities outweigh challenges in the Sahara desert, so I disagree with the statement in the question. As technology continues to develop, there will be more ways to tackle these challenges, but the climate crisis could make the challenge of high temperatures and water shortages more severe in the future.

Look out for spelling, punctuation and grammar marks on longer 9-mark questions. This includes geographical terms. 3 marks could be equivalent to one third of a grade on this paper. See mark scheme on page 179.

DESERTIFICATION

Desertification happens when previously fertile land becomes desert. It is more serious than the land becoming dry during a drought as it won't reverse unless action is taken.

Areas on the fringe (edge) of hot deserts are at risk of desertification and nearly a fifth of land in the world is facing this threat.

Causes of desertification

Climate change

As the global climate changes, temperatures in deserts are increasing and rainfall is becoming more unreliable. When rain falls it is intense and washes away soil, whilst very high temperatures and long dry periods make it difficult for vegetation to grow.

Population growth

Fertility rates tend to be higher in low income countries (LICs) and decrease as a country develops. Areas on the edges of deserts are often less developed and so have rapid population growth, meaning demand for food and fuel is increasing.

Removal of fuel wood

People in LICs often rely on wood for fuel, particularly in remote areas. When trees and bushes are cut down the soil is easily eroded by wind or during intense rainfall.

Overgrazing

Farmers keen to feed their families may try to graze their herds in the same area for longer, removing the vegetation and leaving the soil exposed to erosion.

Over-cultivation

If farmers grow crops on land for too many years without leaving the land fallow (unused) for a year or rotating crops the soil will become infertile.

Soil erosion

A lack of vegetation exposes the soil, which can then be removed by wind and water, leaving desert conditions behind.

Strategies used to reduce the risk of desertification

Desertification can be managed through:

- Water and soil management
- Tree planting
- Use of appropriate technology

Most schemes to tackle desertification use a combination of these strategies to maximise their benefit.

Planting mango trees holds soil together and provides fruit for people.

The Great Green Wall

When the **Great Green Wall** was proposed to tackle desertification in the Sahel, on the fringe of the Sahara desert, the plan was to plant a wall of trees 15 km wide for a distance of 8000 km. Once the planting started, up to 80% of the trees died within two months as they were in remote areas and so not cared for and didn't have enough water.

The plan was reviewed, focusing on:

- Water harvesting – collecting, storing and using rain water
- Agroforestry – growing trees and crops on the same land
- Regenerative agriculture – farming that improves the soil and retention of water which in turn stores carbon and so mitigates climate change (links to earlier climate change topic).

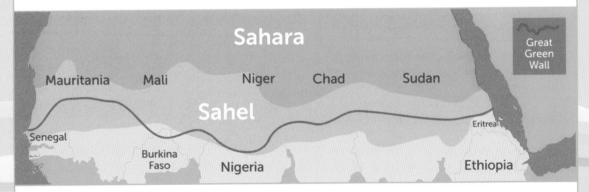

Local farmers in each country are asked for advice about what will work in their area. In Burkina Faso farmers explained how to use zai – pits dug in the soil before planting crops to capture rainfall, sometimes with manure added to attract termites which keep the soil in good condition. This improves crop yields and the quality of the soil. Digging zai is an example of appropriate technology – it is a simple, affordable technique which improves peoples' lives. Indigenous people also advise on which specific trees should be planted in which strategic locations.

Whilst this approach hasn't created the Great Green Wall originally planned, it has been successful in tackling desertification.

'Human activity creates both the causes of and the solutions for desertification.'
To what extent do you agree with this statement? [9]

I strongly agree with this statement as human activity is behind all of the causes of desertification, but people also have the ideas and resources to tackle this problem.

Desertification happens when land that was fertile turns into desert. One reason for this change is the climate emergency, which is leading to higher temperatures and increasingly unreliable rainfall in areas on the fringe of deserts, such as the Sahel. As the climate becomes more extreme the vegetation struggles to grow, leaving soils exposed to soil erosion, leading to desertification. The natural greenhouse effect has been enhanced by human activity, including burning fossil fuels, causing the climate crisis. Growing populations in countries in the Sahel puts pressure on farmers to maximise their yields, which can lead to overcultivation and over grazing, leaving the soil infertile and prone to erosion. Demand for wood for fuel exacerbates this.

Whilst human activity undoubtedly causes desertification, human activity can also bring solutions, restoring land which had become desert. An example is the Great Green Wall of Africa which runs through the Sahel. Water harvesting techniques are used to catch and store rainwater which is then used to grow a mixture of trees and crops (agroforestry). Advice from indigenous farmers is used to make sure the right species of native trees are planted in the most effective locations in each area, maximising their likelihood of survival. Restorative farming is used to return the soil to health and appropriate technology such as digging zai pits in Burkina Faso supports this.

In conclusion, I strongly agree that human activity creates both the causes of and the solutions for desertification. A combination of traditional forestry and farming techniques with new technology can make a major difference in areas such as the Sahel.

This levels-based question should be marked in accordance with the mark bands provided on page 179.

HOT DESERT PLANT AND ANIMAL ADAPTATIONS

Plant adaptations

Plants have **adapted** to the extreme environment. **Xerophytes** are plants that survive in hot, dry conditions.

- Cacti have waxy skin and spikes rather than leaves to reduce **evapotranspiration**. A long tap root helps them reach water deep below the surface.
- The prickly pear plant stores water in its fleshy leaf pads.
- Some desert plants are **dormant** when it is dry, only flowering and reproducing when it rains.

Animal adaptations

Animals have also adapted to the desert environment. Many are **nocturnal**, becoming active during the night time when it is cooler. Some are cold blooded, relying on the heat of the sun to give them energy.

An example of an animal which has adapted to life in the desert is a camel:

- Camels store fat in their humps and lose little water through urination and perspiration.
- They have two rows of eyelashes and narrow nostrils to avoid sand getting into their eyes and nose.
- Their knees have thick, padded skin so they aren't damaged when kneeling on gravel and rocks, and their wide, padded feet are protected from heat and sharp surfaces.

Using the photograph on the left, explain how plants have adapted to the desert environment. [4]

The vegetation shown in the background is low lying and scrubby as the climate is dry, meaning plants need to conserve water and grow slowly. The ground between plants is bare as it is too dry for leafy plants such as grass to grow. The cactus in the foreground has spikes rather than leaves and a waxy surface to reduce evaporation. It is likely to have a long tap root so that it can reach water below the surface. See page 178.

⭐ This photograph shows part of the landscape in the Joshua Tree National Park in the USA. GCSE geographers are often asked to describe and explain what they can see in a photograph. Think about what you can see in the foreground and the background and make explicit use of the photograph.

COLD ENVIRONMENT CHARACTERISTICS

Cold environments (tundra and polar) are cold all year round as there is little insolation (heating from the sun) at the poles. They are dry because of the high pressure.

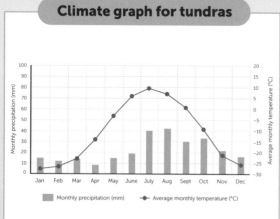

Climate graph for tundras

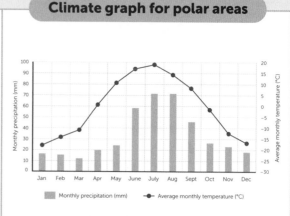

Climate graph for polar areas

Revisit your work on the global atmospheric circulation system on page 13.

Interdependence of climate, water, soils, plants, animals and people

Polar environments are found at and around the poles and are extremely cold and dry. Temperatures fall as low as −50°C and precipitation falls as snow. Soils are usually frozen; if the ground has been frozen for two or more years it is known as **permafrost**. This means there is very low biodiversity, with only a little lichen and moss at the edge of the ice and a few animals who have adapted to this harsh habitat. Indigenous people are often nomadic, moving to scarce resources and surviving due to their deep understanding of the polar ecosystem.

In contrast, **tundra environments** are found at lower latitudes and have temperatures which may drop below −20°C in winter but are much milder in the summer. Frozen soils melt on the surface in the summer but remain frozen deeper down (permafrost). Biodiversity is greater than in polar areas, but is still low, with plants adapted to the low temperatures and low growing. The quality of soil is affected by the lack of plants as there is little to decompose. Low temperatures slow this process, leading to low fertility. Birds and insects thrive in tundra areas in the summer. These areas were once only home to indigenous people who survived by fishing and hunting, but now there are often permanent settlements related to the oil industry. People who have moved into tundra environments may not understand the fragile ecosystem and may use it in unsustainable ways.

Polar

Tundra

Plant and animal adaptations

Very few plants can survive in a **polar** environment, only lichen and moss, as shown in this photograph of a rock in the Arctic.

Plants in **tundra regions** are usually low growing. Some have padded leaves for protection in the strong, dry winds. Others have hairy stems to keep them warm and waxy surfaces to reduce evaporation. Arctic cotton grass, shown, is a type of sedge and uses the adaptations of being low growing and having small seeds which are easily dispersed by the wind. The leaves are thin to reduce evaporation. This grass grows quickly and produces seeds when temperatures warm up in the short summer.

Animals survive in **polar regions** by eating sea creatures such as fish and seals. Polar bears use thick fur and a layer of fat to keep them insulated in the cold Arctic environment.

There is more food in **tundra regions**, so greater biodiversity. Arctic hares have short ears and limbs, and thick fur to keep them warm.

Polar moss and lichen.

Arctic cotton grass.

1. Explain why biodiversity is low in cold environments. [3]
2. Using the photographs of Arctic foxes in winter and summer, opposite, explain how animals have adapted to cold environments. [4]

1. *Cold environments such as tundra environments are cold and dry, with most water stored as ice, which makes it difficult for plants to grow.[1] This means there is little organic matter to enrich soil[1] and also few producers for consumers to eat.[1]*

2. *Arctic foxes have thick fur in the winter to keep them warm. This fur is white so that they blend in with the snowy landscape. They shed their coat for the milder summer, growing thinner darker fur. Their muzzle, ears and legs are short to conserve heat and their thick tail also helps to keep them warm.* Mark in accordance with the mark bands provided on page 178.

CASE STUDY   SVALBARD

Development of cold environments

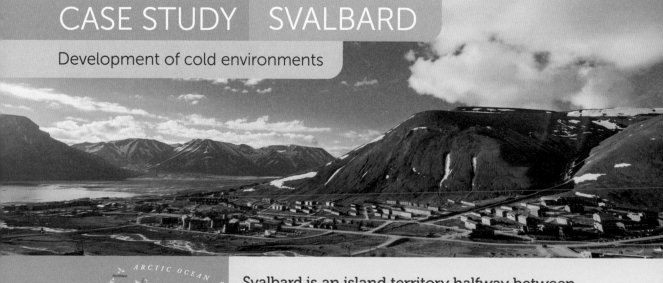

Svalbard is an island territory halfway between Norway and the North Pole. It includes both polar and tundra environments.

The only land mammals are Svalbard reindeer, mountain fox and mice, but there are also around 3000 polar bears. No indigenous people live in Svalbard as it is too far north, but, for around 500 years, it has had temporary huts for people who are there to fish and hunt.

Svalbard became part of Norway when the Svalbard Treaty was signed in the 1920s. People from all of the countries that signed the Treaty are allowed to do business there, but people don't settle permanently; the average time people live in Svalbard is 7 years. The main settlement, Longyearbyen, is home to around 2400 people from around 50 different countries.

Development opportunities in Svalbard

Mineral extraction

Over 300 people are employed in coal mining.

Energy

The Longyearbyen coal fired power station produces electricity for the whole of Svalbard.

Fishing

Russia and Norway control fishing in the Barents Sea.

Tourism

Tourists visit Svalbard to see the fjords, glaciers and wildlife, and to take part in adventure tourism. The harbour at Longyearbyen has been enlarged to cope with visits from cruise ships. Tourism provides around 300 jobs.

Using a case study, to what extent do challenges outweigh the opportunities for development in a cold environment?   [9 marks] + [3 SPaG]

Although there are significant challenges in developing the island territory of Svalbard, people have settled in this area and are exploiting the opportunities of the landscape.

Despite the challenge of transporting machinery, materials and people into such remote areas, a coal mine was established in the early 1900s and the town of Longyearbyen developed. Temperatures in the town can drop below -30°C and the ground is frozen, but people have overcome this by wearing layers of clothes and building homes raised above the ground. Coal from the mines is burnt to make electricity to heat homes and power industry in Svalbard. There is a thriving fishing industry in the Barents Sea, but no food can be grown in Svalbard, so all other food is imported.

Both the coal and tourism industries employ around 300 people in Svalbard. Whilst the coal industry may not survive in the long term as people seek renewable, less polluting alternatives, the tourism industry in Svalbard may mean the settlement of Longyearbyen continues to exist in the future. Tourists often arrive on cruise ships, keen to see the fjords and to take part in adventurous activities such as kayaking and snowmobiling.

People are overcoming the challenges in Svalbard so that they can exploit the opportunities, but the average time people stay in the area is only seven years, suggesting that the environment is too extreme for permanent settlement. Coal mining was the initial reason for settlement in Svalbard and we are yet to see if people to continue to live there as the mines close. Currently, the opportunities for development in Svalbard outweigh the challenges, but this may not always be the case.

Level 3 – Detailed: 9 marks
SPaG – 3 marks: Accurate use of spelling and grammar, including a wide range of geographical terms.

Challenges

There are many challenges facing people living and working in Svalbard including:

Extreme temperatures

People have to dress in layers of warm clothes to protect against frostbite, making it difficult to work outside. Temperatures in Longyearbyen can drop below −30°C. Most work outside but construction is limited to the short summer when there is more daylight, and it is warmer.

Buildings and infrastructure

If buildings and pipes are built on or under the ground they may melt the permafrost, so the ground must be protected.

Inaccessibility

Svalbard is reached by plane and ship, with few roads outside Longyearbyen. Snowmobiles are used to travel around.

Look out for spelling, punctuation and grammar marks on longer 9-mark questions. This includes geographical terms. 3 marks could be equivalent to one third of a grade on this paper.

RISKS TO COLD ENVIRONMENTS FROM ECONOMIC DEVELOPMENT

Cold environments are valuable as **wildernesses** since they are relatively untouched by human activity.

These environments are **fragile** as species have adapted to fit into a particular environmental niche and are unable to cope with rapid changes in their habitat. It takes a long time for plants to grow in the cold conditions, so damage to vegetation takes a long time to repair itself.

Climate change

Climate change has led to Arctic temperatures increasing twice as fast as in other places, but many cold environments are also threatened at a local scale by activities such as coal **mining** and off road driving.

Indigenous groups

The way of life of indigenous people in tundra areas is under threat as people such as Inuit face both climate change and globalisation.

An Inuit man with his son. Adopting a western lifestyle brings benefits, but traditions are lost.

Environmental issues

Damaging cold environments has widespread effects. For example, **overfishing** in Arctic waters affects global fish numbers as many species **migrate** to Arctic waters to spawn (lay eggs). As ice on Arctic lakes melts, methane produced by rotting vegetation in the lakes is released, enhancing the greenhouse effect.

Strategies to balance development and conservation

The challenge facing leaders in cold environments is how to balance the needs of development with the conservation of the fragile environment.

Use of technology	Role of governments	International agreements
The Trans-Alaskan Pipeline (shown overleaf) transports oil from its source to an ice free port 1300km away. In some places it is hidden underground and in others it is raised up to prevent melting of permafrost and to let caribou migrate.	Alaska's environment is protected by the National Environmental Policy Act passed in the US in the 1960s. 9 million hectares of wilderness is protected by the Western Arctic Reserve.	Twelve countries signed the Antarctic Treaty in 1959, agreeing that Antarctica can only be used for peaceful purposes, will have freedom of scientific investigation and that findings from research shall be exchanged and made freely available. 54 countries have now signed the treaty.

Use of technology

An example of a non-governmental organisation (NGO) working in conservation in a cold environment is Greenpeace. Their icebreaking scientific research ship, Arctic Sunrise, has been used to document evidence of oil pollution of marine environments and to conduct scientific research into biodiversity in Antarctica.

'Human activity can both damage and conserve fragile cold environments.'
To what extent do you agree with this statement? [9]

I strongly agree with this statement as human activity can easily damage fragile cold environments, but people also have the ideas and resources to tackle this problem and conserve these areas of wilderness.

Svalbard was originally developed so that people could mine coal and has since become a tourist destination. This island in the Arctic Ocean was previously uninhabited and is home to around 3000 polar bears who roam the wilderness. Coal mining has caused damage to the local habitat, but burning coal is having a much wider effect on Arctic environments as the enhanced greenhouse effect is causing the Arctic to warm up at twice the rate of other places. Animals such as Svalbard reindeer have adapted to the environmental niche of the islands but are now struggling to adapt to the rapid change in temperatures.

Tourist numbers in Svalbard have increased as more people have become interested in adventure tourism and visiting wilderness locations. This has led to the harbour at Longyearbyen being extended. Tourists can damage the fragile environment as they head into the wilderness on snowmobiles.

However, people also have the answers to tackling the problems faced in cold environments. International agreements such as the Antarctic Treaty show that countries can make joint decisions to protect wilderness environments. The Antarctic Treaty ensures the continent is used for peaceful reasons and that scientific findings are shared.

This shows that people can both damage and conserve fragile cold environments, but the problem is that people in power may see the value of developing resources as more significant than the value of these environments as natural wildernesses. Refer to levels-based mark scheme on page 179.

EXAMINATION PRACTICE

In this section, you should study and revise ecosystems, tropical rainforests and one from hot deserts or cold environments.

1. Study the world map showing the main biomes on **page 29**. Using this map, which one of the following statements is true? [1]

   A. ☐ There is more taiga in the Southern Hemisphere than in the Northern Hemisphere

   B. ☐ Deserts are found along the Equator

   C. ☐ There are no deserts in Asia

   D. ☐ There are areas of mixed and deciduous forest in six of the seven continents

2. Outline **one** reason for the distribution of deserts. [2]

Tropical rainforests

3. Study the climate graph for a tropical rainforest on **page 31**. What is the range of temperature shown? [1]

4. Study the climate graph for a tropical rainforest on **page 31**. In which month is rainfall the lowest? [1]

5. To what extent do you agree that the economic benefits of development are greater than the environmental costs in a tropical rainforest you have studied? [9]

Hot deserts option

6. Outline **one** distinctive characteristic of the desert climate. [1]

7. Study the photographs showing uses of the Sahara desert below and on **pages 38–39**. Using at least one of these photographs and your own understanding, explain how deserts can be used in more and less sustainable ways. [6]

A room in an ecological hotel in Siwa, Egypt

Desert caves in the Matmata region of Berbers in Tunisia

8. Study the photograph showing mango trees being planted and cared for on **page 41**. Using this photograph, suggest how planting trees can reduce the risk of desertification. [2]

9. Outline how **either** water and soil management **or** appropriate technology can reduce the risk of desertification. [2]

Cold environments option

10. Give **one** reason why cold environments are so cold. [1]

11. Study the photographs below. Using at least one of these photographs and your own understanding, explain how cold environments can be used in more and less sustainable ways. [6]

12. Study the photograph showing the Trans Alaskan pipeline below.
Using this photograph, suggest **one** way in which technology can be used to conserve cold environments. [2]

13. Explain how international treaties reduce the risk of damage in cold environments. [2]

UK PHYSICAL LANDSCAPES

The UK has a range of diverse landscapes, including major **upland** and **lowland** areas, and **river systems**. Landscapes are created by the interaction of natural processes and human activity.

Topographical map of the UK

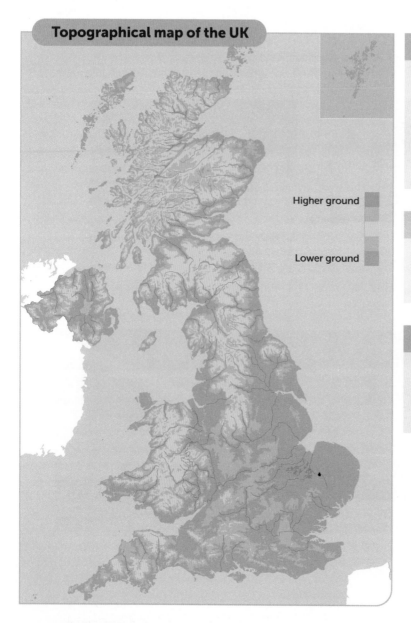

Higher ground

Lower ground

Upland areas

Highland areas are mainly found in the north and the west of the UK. This is because the geology of these areas consists of resistant rocks such as slate and granite.

Rivers

Most rivers in the UK have their source in the mountains and flow to the sea.

Lowland areas

Low lying areas are found in the south and east of the UK where the rocks are less resistant.

In this section, you are expected to study UK physical landscapes and **two** options from Coastal, River or Glacial landscapes in the UK.

Using the map on this page and an example, describe the distribution of highland areas in the UK. [2]

Highland areas are mainly found in the north and west of the UK.[1] // or the absence of higher ground in eastern England.[1] Example high ground is the Grampian Mountain range in Scotland.[1]

COASTAL LANDSCAPES IN THE UK

Coastal landscapes are found where the land meets the sea. They are shaped by a combination of natural and human processes.

Wave types and characteristics

Waves form when wind blows over water, forming ripples in the surface. The size of waves is affected by the strength of the wind and the **fetch**. The fetch is the distance the wave travels whilst being blown by the wind.

Waves start to interact with the seafloor as they get near to the coast, at which point they will break. Water rushes up the beach as the **swash** and then runs back into the sea as **backwash**.

The diagram below shows the two main types of waves.

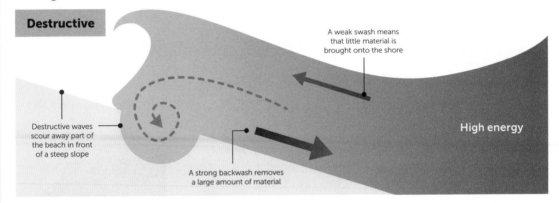

Destructive

A weak swash means that little material is brought onto the shore

Destructive waves scour away part of the beach in front of a steep slope

A strong backwash removes a large amount of material

High energy

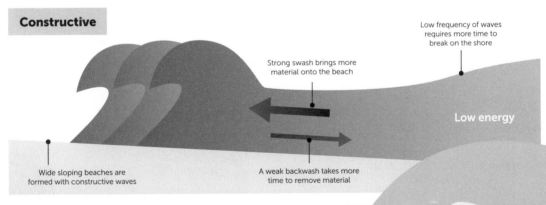

Constructive

Low frequency of waves requires more time to break on the shore

Strong swash brings more material onto the beach

Wide sloping beaches are formed with constructive waves

A weak backwash takes more time to remove material

Low energy

COASTAL PROCESSES

Weathering processes

Weathering processes break rocks down without moving them away.

Mechanical weathering

Mechanical (or physical) weathering breaks down rock through processes such as freeze-thaw weathering. Water in cracks in rock freezes at night, expanding the cracks, then thaws in the day. Over time pieces of rock will break off and fall to the ground to form a scree slope.

Chemical weathering

Chemical weathering involves a chemical reaction. An example is carbonation, where water which is slightly acidic because it has absorbed CO_2 slowly dissolves alkaline rocks such as limestone.

Mass movement

Mass movement occurs when weathered material, e.g. rock, falls due to gravity.

Sliding

Blocks of material slide down along their bedding planes.

Rock falls

Rock breaks off and falls, often due to freeze-thaw weathering.

Slumping

Unconsolidated rock (loose pieces) and soil falls in a curving motion (rotational).

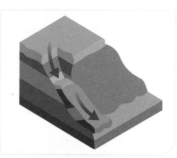

Erosion

Erosion wears away and removes material.

Abrasion

Material carried in waves wears the coastline away.

Attrition

Pieces of material carried in waves knock against each other, becoming smaller and rounder over time.

Hydraulic power

Water hits the coastline, creates high air pressure in cracks which breaks pieces off into the water.

Waves erode the Jurassic Coast in Dorset

Transportation

Transportation moves material along the coast.

Longshore drift

Drift happens when waves approach the coastline at an angle, as shown here in the diagram.

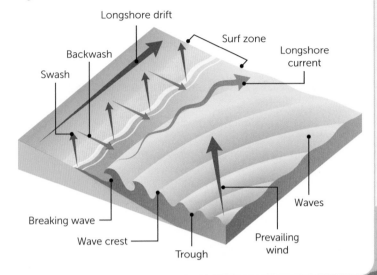

Deposition

Deposition occurs when material is dropped by the waves. This happens when waves have less energy such as in bays and estuaries.

Describe the characteristics of a constructive wave. [3]

Constructive waves are low energy waves[1] with a strong swash[1] and a weak backwash.[1]

DISTINCTIVE COASTAL LANDFORMS

Coastal landforms are created by the action of physical processes. They vary according to the nature of the coastline, with geological structure and rock type playing an important role.

Influence of geological structure and rock type

Geological structure

Geological structure refers to the way the rocks in the coastline fit together. Sedimentary rocks are laid down in layers, but these layers may change over time due to the movement of the Earth through:

Faulting

Cracks in the layers along lines of weakness.

Folding

Layers are tilted (see photograph above).

Rock type

Rock type varies around the UK coastline. Rocks such as granite, slate and limestone are more resistant to erosion, whereas clays and sands are less resistant to erosion. In areas with coastlines made from glacial deposits (such as till) the material is unconsolidated (loose) so it is easily eroded.

This photograph shows a cliff on the Norfolk coastline. This coastline consists of sand, clay and glacial till, so the cliffs are rapidly eroded.

The photograph shows Old Harry Rocks in Dorset. Explain how landforms like this form. [4]

The photograph shows an arch and a stack. These have formed in a headland when processes such as hydraulic action and abrasion[1] have eroded a weak point such as a crack.[1] If a crack widens to form a cave and the cave cuts through the headland an arch will form.[1] When the roof of the arch collapses it forms a stack like Old Harry.[1]

Landforms of erosion

Headlands and bays

Headlands and **bays** often form on discordant coastlines. This is when there are bands of more and less resistant rock, as shown in the diagram.

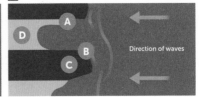

Soft (less resistant) rock such as: Clay, sands, gravels   Hard (more resistant) rock such as: Chalk, limestone

Direction of waves

Direction of waves

A Once formed, bays are then sheltered by the headlands so their erosion is slowed down

B Once formed, headlands are more likely to be eroded as the energy of the waves become focused here

C Headlands remain jutting out as they erode more slowly

D The less resistant rocks erode more quickly, forming bays

Cliffs and wave cut platforms

Cliffs and **wave cut platforms** are formed when:

1 The base of the cliff is eroded through hydraulic action and abrasion forming a wave cut notch.

2 Eventually the rock above the notch will fall (mass movement) and the cliff will move back (retreat).

3 This leaves behind a wave cut platform (where the cliff used to be).

Example

This photograph shows the cliff and wave cut platform at Kilve Beach in Somerset.

The base of the limestone cliffs is eroded, forming a wave cut notch. The limestone in the cliffs is strong enough to stay up when it is undercut. You can also see the folding of the rock in the cliffs in the photograph, which influences how erosion affects this coastline. Eventually the cliff will collapse, leaving behind a wave cut platform.

Caves, arches and stacks

Caves, **arches** and **stacks** can form when headlands are eroded, as shown in the diagram.

Cliff retreats in this direction

6 Collapsed arch leaves behind a tall stack

Headland

Abrasion and continued hydraulic action cause the crack to grow

Cave continues to grow

2

3

4

5 Arch is eroded and eventually collapses

7

1 Large crack caused by the action of the waves

Natural arch is formed when the cave breaks through the headland

Stack is eroded to form a stump

LANDFORMS OF DEPOSITION

Types of beaches

Sandy beaches

Sandy **beaches** form in sheltered bays when sand is deposited. The sheltered nature means the sand isn't washed away.

Pebble beaches

Pebble **beaches** can form on higher energy coastlines as it takes more energy to move pebbles than sand.

Sand dunes

Sand dunes develop in coastal areas where there is a supply of sand which is blown inland. Embryo dunes form when the wind-blown sand meets an obstacle and is deposited. These dunes may be blown or washed away, or they may become stabilised as plants such as sea couch grass grow on them. Dunes further from the sea have a surface layer of soil (as vegetation has decomposed and mixed with the sand) and a wider range of species of vegetation. This change in sand dunes is known as succession and is shown in the diagram below.

Spits and bars

Spits and bars are formed through the process of longshore drift when a beach meets a river or the coastline changes shape. Spits are depositional landforms that extend out to sea. The beach at Torcross in Devon (shown below) has extended across a bay, creating a bar. A freshwater lagoon has formed behind the bar.

SWANAGE, DORSET

An example of a section of coastline in the UK

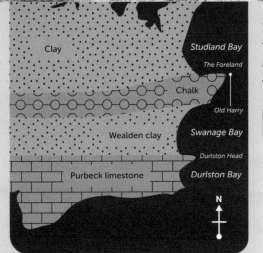

Clay

Studland Bay

The Foreland

Chalk

Old Harry

Wealden clay

Swanage Bay

Durlston Head

Durlston Bay

Purbeck limestone

N

Swanage lies on the Jurassic Coast which runs through Dorset and into Devon. As the diagram shows, this coastline is discordant, with bands of more and less resistant rock.

Landforms of erosion

Studland Bay and Swanage Bay have formed where clays have been eroded, whilst the more resistant chalk and limestone at The Foreland and Durlston Head have eroded more slowly, forming **headlands**.

If you look carefully at the map, you can see Old Harry Rocks (as shown in the photograph on **page 56**) on the end of The Foreland. This rock formation includes an **arch** and a **stack** and formed as the headland was eroded.

Landforms of deposition

Studland Bay is known for its golden **sandy beaches** and **dunes**. The photograph (top) shows the dunes at Shell Bay, where the fine sand has been stabilised by marram grass. Studland Bay also has areas of mudflats and saltmarshes which have developed in the sheltered conditions.

Swanage itself has a wide sandy beach which is popular with tourists.

Using an example, explain how different coastal landforms are formed by erosion. [6]

The Swanage coastline is well known for its landforms of erosion, including Swanage Bay and Old Harry Rocks. Swanage Bay has formed on this discordant coastline as a band of clay has been eroded more rapidly by the action of waves than the bands of chalk and limestone either side of it. Old Harry Rocks formed due to hydraulic action and abrasion eroding The Foreland, which is a headland. Cracks in the chalk rocks widened to form caves, then some of these caves eroded through the headland to form arches. When the roof of arches collapse, stacks form, such as Old Harry.

This levels-based question should be marked in accordance with the mark bands provided on page 178.

COASTAL MANAGEMENT STRATEGIES

Coastal management strategies bring people involved with coastlines together in an attempt to reduce conflicts between different users and to manage the impacts of **physical processes** such as coastal erosion and flooding.

Shoreline Management Plans

The **Environment Agency** works with landowners and others along coastlines in England to produce Shoreline Management Plans (SMPs) for every stretch of coastline. If erosion or flooding is causing concern in an area, a **cost benefit analysis** will be carried out and decisions made about whether to defend the coastline and what methods to use.

Management strategies may involve **hard engineering**, **soft engineering** or **managed retreat**. Often a combination of strategies is used along one stretch of coastline.

Hard engineering

This involves structures being built to control the impact of processes on the coastline.

Gabions

Metal cages are filled with small rocks and used to construct a barrier. They are much cheaper than sea walls and rock armour and sometimes become part of the landscape when vegetation covers them, but the cages can rust in 5–10 years, which is dangerous if they are in areas where people walk or children might play.

Groynes

Wooden or concrete barriers are built at right angles to the beach to trap material being moved by longshore drift and build up the beach so that it protects the coastline. These are also less expensive than sea walls and rock armour and a wider beach may benefit the tourism industry, however, reducing longshore drift may starve beaches further along the coastline of sediment.

Sea walls

Sea walls form a barrier between the land and the sea. Wave return walls are curved to reduce the likelihood of waves breaking over the wall. Sea walls are usually effective and can be part of pleasant promenades, but they are expensive to build and maintain, and look unnatural.

Rock armour

Large rocks are piled up to form a barrier, dissipating the energy of the waves to protect the coastline. Rock armour is cheaper than sea walls and looks more natural, but the rocks are quarried and transported to the coastline which costs money and means they may not match the local geology.

Soft engineering

Natural processes are used to protect the coastline from flooding and erosion.

Beach nourishment and reprofiling

Material is dredged up from the seabed and deposited on the beach (nourishment) and then shaped by bulldozers (reprofiling) to make the beach wider and higher so that land behind it is protected. This looks natural and is popular with tourists, but storms may move the material back out to sea, meaning the process of nourishment will have to be repeated. Reprofiling needs to be carried out regularly to maintain the high, wide beach.

Dune regeneration

Sand dunes provide a natural barrier along some sections of coastline, but they can be damaged during storms or due to human activity. Marram grass can be planted on dunes to stabilise them and damaged areas fenced off to allow them to recover. This is a cheap and natural approach, but is only useful in areas with sand dunes and requires regular monitoring of the condition of the dunes.

Managed retreat

This involves making a decision to let part of the coastline retreat due to flooding or erosion.

Coastal realignment

Coastal realignment involves careful monitoring of the coastline to see how marine processes affect the area. People owning land in these areas have to adapt to the change in the coastline.

In Porlock Bay in Somerset, coastal realignment has meant that fields that used to be farmed have now become salt marshes, as you can see in the photograph. The farmer has less land to use, but the salt marsh is a valuable habitat for birds.

Salt marsh

BURNHAM ON SEA, SOMERSET

An example of a coastal management scheme in the UK

Burnham on Sea is a town on the north Somerset coast. A wide range of coastal management strategies are used along this section of coast.

Reasons for management

In December 1981 a storm hit the sea front at Burnham on Sea. The sea wall was badly damaged, pavements were ripped up and 400 properties flooded.

The management strategy

The new sea wall shown in the photograph was opened in 1986. This 3.2m high wave return wall protects 1.6 km of coastline and cost £7.5 million. The shoreline management plan in this area says 'hold the line' which means that the coast should be defended.

To the north of Burnham on Sea, the village of Berrow is protected by sand dunes. A volunteer group monitors the dunes and uses sand fences to fill any gaps like the one shown in the photograph. Two wire fences are built, with pieces of blackthorn (which grows on the dunes) or even old Christmas trees placed in between. Within six months deposition has covered the fences in sand and they look like the other dunes.

Groynes were once used at Berrow, but they reduced the sand on the beach at Brean, nearby, and so were abandoned.

Further north are the holiday parks and village of Brean. Rock armour, which cost £2.15 million, is used to protect a 1.4 km length of the coastline here from flooding. The picture opposite shows how flat the land is along this stretch of coastline.

The resulting effects and conflicts

The coastal defence strategy has been successful in protecting this area from coastal flooding. The height of the sea wall means that it blocks views of the sea from the town which upset some residents, but the wall was designed to include seating areas which benefit tourists. This low-lying coastline is particularly vulnerable to sea level rise due to climate change, and a higher sea wall may be needed in the next 30 years. The sea wall needs regular maintenance as localised damage is caused during storms.

Sea defences at Scarborough, North Yorkshire

Using the photograph of coastal defences at Scarborough and your own knowledge, explain how the coastline can be protected from physical processes. [6]

The photograph shows rock armour against a sea wall. This is a hard engineering approach, making a barrier between the sea and the coast. Energy in the waves hitting the rock armour will be dispersed, protecting the sea wall from damage. The sea wall provides a barrier but if spray goes over the wall it can run back to the sea through the holes shown in the picture. A similar approach has been used to defend the coastline at Burnham on Sea, where the sea wall has concrete steps in front of it to dissipate the energy of the breaking waves. Further along this coastline, soft engineering is used in the form of dune regeneration. Both these techniques protect the coast from flooding.

This levels-based question should be marked in accordance with the mark bands provided on page 178.

CHANGES IN RIVER VALLEYS FROM SOURCE TO MOUTH

The **source** of most rivers in the UK is in the highland areas. The area of land from which water runs into a river is known as its **drainage basin**, the edge of which is the **watershed** (shown by the dashed line on the diagram on the right).

You are expected to study UK physical landscapes and **two** options from Coastal, River or Glacial landscapes in the UK.

Long and cross profiles

The **long profile** of a river valley shows how it changes as the river flows from source to mouth. A **cross profile** shows the cross section across a river valley. The diagram opposite shows how the river valley changes along both long and cross profiles as it flows from its source to mouth.

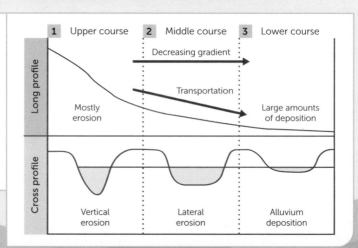

Fluvial processes

Erosion

- **Hydraulic action** – Water wears away the river's banks and bed.
- **Abrasion** – Material carried by the water wears away the banks and bed.
- **Attrition** – Material carried by the water wears away other material, making it smaller and rounder.
- **Solution** – Alkaline rocks are dissolved by the weak acid in river water.
- **Vertical erosion** – the river cuts down and the valley becomes deeper.
- **Lateral erosion** – the river cuts sideways and the valley becomes wider.

Transportation

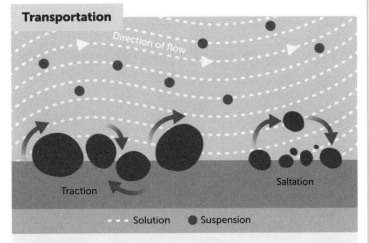

Direction of flow

Traction

Saltation

- - - Solution ● Suspension

- **Traction** – larger material moves along the riverbed.
- **Saltation** – material moves through a combination of movement along the bed and floating in the current sometimes described as a leap frogging motion.
- **Suspension** – smaller material floats along in the current.
- **Solution** – dissolved material moving as part of the flow of water.

Deposition

When a river has less energy, it will drop its load (the material it is carrying). This happens on the inside of the bend in meanders and in the lower course of a river as it gets close to its mouth.

Describe how a river valley changes as the river flows downstream. [4]

In the upper course of the river, near the source, the river flows through a V-shaped valley, but as the river flows into the middle course of the river the river gets wider and the valley sides are less steep. In the lower course of the river the valley flattens out, forming a flood plain.

This levels-based question should be marked in accordance with the mark bands provided on page 178.

FLUVIAL LANDFORMS

Physical processes combine to create different **fluvial landforms** along the course of river.

Landforms resulting from erosion

Waterfalls

Waterfalls form on rivers for several reasons, but probably the best known is when rivers flow from an area of more resistant rock to an area of less resistant rock, as shown in the diagrams.

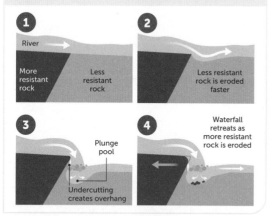

Gorges

As waterfalls retreat, they cut a narrow, steep sided valley known as a gorge.

Interlocking spurs

An interlocking spur results when rivers wind between hills (resistant rock).

Landforms resulting from erosion and deposition

Meanders

These bends in the river are constantly changing shape due to erosion and deposition. The water flows fastest on the outside of the bend, so this is where erosion happens and a river cliff forms, as can be seen in the photograph. The slower current on the inside of the bend leads to deposition and the formation of a slip off slope.

Ox-bow lakes

If the neck of a meander is eroded, an ox-bow lake may form, as is shown in the diagram.

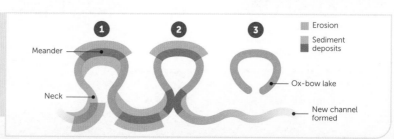

Landforms resulting from deposition

Levees

When a river floods the largest material is deposited first, building up a natural embankment. Levees grow as more material is added in future floods.

Estuaries

Where a river meets the sea, it deposits the load it is carrying, which may form mudflats and saltmarshes if the material isn't washed away by waves and tides.

Flood plains

As meanders move downstream over time, they carve out a flat area of land which is then covered in silt each time the river floods.

Using the photograph and your own knowledge, explain how meanders change over time. [4]

The photograph shows that the bank on the outside of the bend has collapsed. This happened because the bank was undercut by the river. The fastest flow of the river is on the outside of the bend, giving it the energy to erode the bank in this way through processes such as hydraulic action.
Level 2 – Detailed: 4 marks. See page 178.

THE RIVER TEES

An example of a river valley in the UK

The source of the River Tees is in the Pennine Hills in the north east of England and its mouth is in the North Sea.

Landforms of deposition

The River Tees meets the North Sea at Middlesbrough. At this **estuary** the mudflats have been drained so that a large industrial site could be developed.

Landforms of erosion

There are many **meanders** in the lower and middle course of the Tees.

The town of Yarm developed in a meander of the river as it was a good defensive position.

High Force waterfall is found in the upper course of the River Tees.

A band of igneous whinstone meets sedimentary limestone. The limestone erodes more rapidly than the whinstone, creating a step in the landscape.

As High Force has retreated, it has formed a **gorge** which is about 700m in length.

1. Study the photograph above of the River Cuckmere in the South Downs National Park.
   Explain how these landforms may change over time .   [6]

2. Look at the OS map extracts below, marked A and B.

© Crown copyright and database rights 2022 OS 100065506

© Crown copyright and database rights 2022 OS 100065506

(a) Which map shows the middle course of the river?   [1]

(b) What is the evidence for this?   [2]

1. *Landforms shown in the photograph include meanders and a floodplain. Meanders migrate over*
    time, with erosion affecting the outside of the bends whilst deposition occurs on the inside. The
    neck of the meander in the foreground of the photograph is narrow. Erosion may break through
    this neck, forming a straighter part of the river and leaving behind an ox bow lake. When the river
    floods it will deposit silt on the floodplain, increasing the depth of soil there.

    This levels-based question should be marked in accordance with the mark bands provided on page 178.

2. *(a) Map A shows the middle course of the river.[1]*
    (b) One mark for each point or two marks for one developed point.
        The land in map B has contour lines close together showing that it is steep[1], whereas the
        land on map A is much flatter.[1]
        Or: The river has a large meander in map A[1] and the land is also much flatter.[1]

MANAGING THE EFFECTS OF FLOODING

River flooding occurs when there is too much water flowing into the river from the drainage basin to fit into the **river channel**. Different **management strategies** can be used to protect river landscapes from the effects of flooding.

Factors affecting flood risk

Precipitation

- If rain is so **intense** (heavy) that it can't **infiltrate** (soak) into the ground fast enough, it will form puddles and run over the surface into rivers, increasing the flood risk.
- If rain has fallen for several days, the ground will be **saturated**, again leading to puddles and surface flow into rivers causing an increased flood risk.
- Precipitation can also fall as snow, which can cause flooding when it melts.

Geology

- Water doesn't infiltrate into **impermeable rocks** such as granite, so it flows rapidly over the rock surface into rivers, which can increase the flood risk.
- **Permeable rocks**, such as sandstone, allow water to pass through, so water travels more slowly to the river as throughflow and groundwater flow. Some water will also be stored underground. This reduces flood risk.

Relief

- Water runs more rapidly down **steep slopes** and is less likely to infiltrate into the ground, meaning that it will reach the river quickly.
- Infiltration is more likely on **gentle slopes**, meaning the flood risk will be reduced.

Land use

- **Forests** intercept precipitation and their vegetation uses water as part of photosynthesis. Evapotranspiration occurs when water evaporates from plants. Trees also hold soil together, preventing it from being washed away. **Deforestation** of an area therefore means more water will reach a river more rapidly by flowing over the surface. Soil erosion can also mean rivers are more likely to flood as they become full of silt which reduces their capacity.
- When an area is **urbanised**, it is covered with impermeable surfaces. Drainage systems will be built to remove water quickly from the settlement, transferring it into rivers. This increases the surrounding flood risk.
- The way **farmers** use the land has an impact on the flood risk. If fields are left bare or if ploughing makes furrows down hills, water will flow more rapidly into rivers, increasing the flood risk.

Hydrographs

Flood or storm hydrographs show the relationship between precipitation and discharge. The bar graph shows how much precipitation has fallen and the line graph shows the discharge in the river. Discharge is the amount of water which passes a certain point in the river in one second. It is measured in cubic metres per second (cumecs).

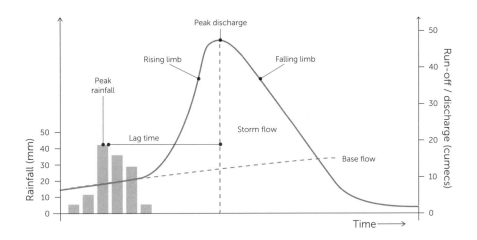

When considering flood risk, it is useful to look at certain elements of the hydrograph:

Lag time

What is the time difference between the peak rainfall and the peak discharge? A short lag time means water is quickly reaching the river, which is likely to increase the flood risk.

Peak discharge

If the peak discharge is greater than the bank full capacity of the river, there will be a flood.

Flood hydrographs vary between different drainage basins and within the same drainage basin over time. Factors influencing the shape of flood hydrographs include basin size, rock type, land use, relief, rainfall intensity and duration, and soil moisture levels.

Explain how urbanisation and deforestation impact lag time and peak discharge. [4]

Urbanisation will mean that the lag time will decrease, and the peak discharge will increase as more water runs quickly into the river over impermeable surfaces and through drains.

Deforestation will also decrease the lag time and increase the peak discharge as less water is being intercepted by trees.

COSTS AND BENEFITS OF RIVER MANAGEMENT STRATEGIES

Hard engineering

Hard engineering means building structures to control flooding.

Dams and reservoirs

Dams hold back water so a reservoir forms behind them, as shown in the photograph of Craig Goch Dam in Powys, Wales. The flow of water over the dam is carefully controlled. Dams can be used for flood control, generating hydroelectric power and water storage. They are expensive to build, and land flooded to form the reservoir can no longer be used.

Flood relief channels

An empty channel may be created next to a river channel, as is shown in the photograph of Exeter. If there is a risk of the city flooding a flood gate can be opened and the flood relief channel will fill, reducing the pressure on the river.

Embankments

Raising riverbanks means a channel has the capacity to hold more water, but habitats are disturbed and if concrete is used it can look unnatural.

Straightening

Making a river channel straighter speeds up the flow of the water, but this can increase the flood risk downstream. Habitats are damaged when a river is straightened, particularly if it is lined with concrete.

Soft engineering

Soft engineering involves working with nature to manage the risk of floods.

Flood warnings and preparation

Precipitation and river discharge are carefully monitored. Warnings are issued if a flood is forecast. Some places have stores of sandbags for people to use to protect doorways.

River restoration

A river which has been managed using hard engineering strategies may be restored so that natural processes can help regulate the river i.e. concrete banks may be removed, wetland areas restored and straightened sections allowed to meander.

Planting trees

Afforestation means more water is intercepted and soil erosion is prevented, reducing the flood risk as well as bringing other environmental benefits.

Flood plain zoning

Development can be restricted in areas with a high risk of flooding. These areas may be used for leisure facilities instead.

SOMERSET COUNTY COUNCIL

An example of a flood management scheme in the UK

Why the scheme was required

As storms crossed Somerset in January and February 2014, they brought record rainfall. The rainwater couldn't soak into the saturated soils, so remained on the surface or flowed into rivers such as the Rivers Parrett and Tone, which hadn't been dredged for 20 years. The storms also caused storm surges, increasing water levels in the tidal sections of the rivers.

600 houses were flooded, 16 farms were evacuated, and the damage was estimated at £147 million. The floodwater mixed with oil and sewage, polluting the environment.

The management strategy

The Environment Agency and Somerset County Council announced a £20 million Flood Action Plan for the Somerset Levels in March 2014.

- 8km of the Rivers Parrett and Tone were dredged before the Autumn of 2014 and the temporary pumping site at Dunball was made permanent.
- Riverbanks were repaired and roads at risk of flooding raised and improved.
- In some areas, wetlands have been restored so that they can absorb precipitation.

Plans for a £99m tidal barrier across the River Parrett in Bridgwater were submitted to the government in 2019.

Explain how hard engineering strategies can help to reduce the impact of flooding. [4]

Dams can be built across a river, meaning that the amount of water allowed to flow downstream can be controlled, reducing the risk of flooding downstream. Riverbanks may be built up using concrete or dredged mud from the river to form embankments which increase the capacity of the river channel and so reduce the flood risk.

Refer to the mark bands provided on page 178.

The social, economic and environmental issues

Social

Residents are more confident that their homes are safe. Raised roads mean communities such as Muchelney are less likely to be cut off and become isolated.

Economic

The scheme costs a large amount of money but protects a large area. Without flood defence work, some people would find it hard to insure and sell their homes on the Levels.

Environmental

Dredging rivers disturbs the river ecosystem and animal habitats.

THE ROLE OF ICE IN SHAPING THE UK

A large part of the UK was covered by ice during the last **ice age**. Valleys carved by **glaciers** in the north and west of the UK are still evident.

You are expected to study UK physical landscapes and **two** options from Coastal, River or Glacial landscapes in the UK.

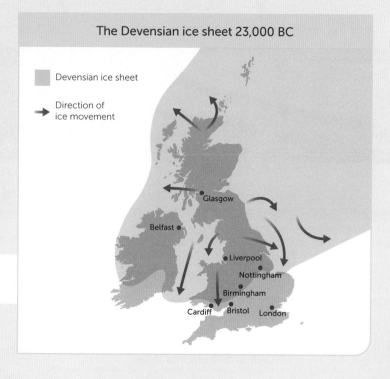

The Devensian ice sheet 23,000 BC

Devensian ice sheet

→ Direction of ice movement

Glasgow
Belfast
Liverpool
Nottingham
Birmingham
Cardiff   Bristol   London

Glacial processes

Freeze-thaw weathering

Water freezes in the winter and thaws in summer. When rock is repeatedly frozen and thawed it will eventually weaken and crack. Pieces fall to the base of the rock to form scree slopes.

Scree slopes in the Lake District

Movement

Glaciers move slowly through **internal deformation** (when a solid flows downhill due to gravity) and more rapidly through **basal slip** (sliding on a layer of meltwater).

The type of movement depends on whether the glacier is frozen to the rock or if there is a layer of meltwater. Glacial ice moving from hollows in mountains may move through **rotational slip** along a curved base.

Vatnajökull glacier, Iceland

Glacial processes continued

Transportation

Material transported by glaciers is known as **moraine** and can be found in, on or below the glacier. When glaciers move down a valley, loose material is pushed in front of them – this is known as **bulldozing**.

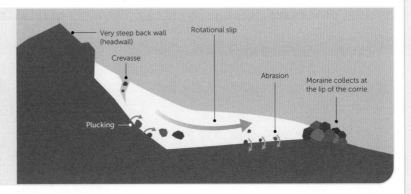

Very steep back wall (headwall)

Rotational slip

Crevasse

Abrasion

Moraine collects at the lip of the corrie

Plucking

Deposition

Glaciers deposit material when they melt. Most material is deposited at the glacier's snout (where all the ice melts).

Till

When piles of material are left behind they are known as **till** or boulder clay. This consists of rocks of mixed sizes and creates the cliffs of unconsolidated material that are so rapidly eroded in some parts of the UK coastline. **See page 56.**

Outwash

Meltwater transports material away from the snout (end) of the glacier, with larger pieces being deposited close to the snout and smaller pieces being carried further away. When gravel and sand is deposited it is known as **outwash**.

Explain how glaciers erode the landscape. [4]

Glaciers may erode the landscape through abrasion as rocks carried within them scrape the valley sides and floor. They may also erode the valley through plucking when meltwater freezes around a rock and then pulls it away as the glacier moves.

This is a levels based question. Refer to the mark bands provided on page 178.

GLACIAL LANDFORMS

Physical processes combine to create different **glacial landforms**.

Landforms resulting from erosion

Corries

Corries form from the rotational movement of glaciers high in a glacial valley as shown in the diagram. They are also known as cirques and cwms.

Truncated spurs

These are interlocking spurs which have been cut through by a glacier. **See page 74.**

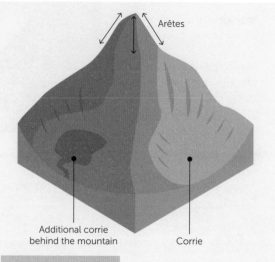

Additional corrie behind the mountain

Corrie

Ribbon lakes

Long narrow bodies of water that form along the bottom of a glacial trough.

Arêtes

Arêtes form when two corries erode back towards each other.

Pyramidal peaks

These form when three corries erode back towards each other.

Hanging valleys

These are created by glaciers cutting through tributaries into a main valley

Glacial troughs

This is a U-shaped valley carved by a glacier.

Landforms resulting from transportation and deposition

Types of moraine

Material carried by glaciers is named according to its position in the glacier.

- **Lateral moraine** forms at the edges.
- **Medial moraine** forms between two glaciers.
- **Ground moraine** is found below glaciers.
- **Terminal moraine** forms at the glacier's snout.

Erratics

Large boulders which have been deposited far from their source by glaciers.

Drumlins

When glaciers move over deposits of till, they may create smooth shaped hills called drumlins.

Side view

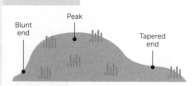

Blunt end

Peak

Tapered end

Plan view

Peak

CADAIR IDRIS, WALES

An example of a glaciated upland area of the UK

Cadair Idris is a mountain in Snowdonia National Park in Wales.

Landforms of erosion	Landforms of deposition
Llyn Cau corrie (shown in the photograph below) is now filled with a **tarn** (lake). The **arête** running along the back of this corrie is called **Craig Cau** and there is also a **pyramidal peak** in this area.	This photograph shows a ribbon lake flowing through the glacial trough at the base of Cadair Idris. The steep sides and flat bottom of the valley are clearly shown.

Study the photograph of Mount Snowdown in Snowdonia National Park in Wales.

Explain how erosional landforms such as these form in glacial areas. [6]

Landforms shown in the photograph include a corrie, arêtes and a pyramidal peak. The corrie in the foreground formed when this area was glaciated. The ice plucked weathered material from the back wall, making it very steep, whilst the rotational movement of the glacier carved a bowl like shape in the mountain through abrasion. The arêtes in the background formed when two corries eroded back towards each other. The pyramidal peak was created by three corries cutting back.

ECONOMIC ACTIVITIES AND MANAGEMENT STRATEGIES IN GLACIATED UPLAND AREAS

Glaciated upland areas provide opportunities for economic activities including tourism, farming, forestry and quarrying, but these areas need to be carefully **managed** to minimise conflict between users and damage to the environment.

Economic activities in glaciated upland areas

Tourism

Tourists are attracted to the scenery and opportunities for adventurous activities in glaciated upland areas. Some areas, such as Aviemore in Scotland, have enough snow to attract skiers in the winter.

Tourism in the Cairngorms, Scotland

Farming

The height of the land and poor soils mean these areas are usually used for sheep farming.

Forestry

There are large plantations of conifers in many upland areas in the UK. These trees grow quickly and are sold as timber.

Quarrying

Certain rocks, valued for construction and industry, may be quarried in glaciated upland areas. One such example is limestone which is quarried in the Peak District and sold for construction and for making lime to add to soils to reduce their acidity.

Conflicts in glaciated upland areas

Between different land uses

Conflicts can occur when people want to make use of the same area in different ways. An example is that livestock can be harmed when tourists walk through their fields with dogs off their leads or leave gates open.

Zip World in North Wales is an example of a business which has tried to balance the needs of development with conservation. The zip lines and underground trampolines have been constructed in an abandoned quarry, so are hidden from view and don't use land in wild areas.

Between development and conservation

Glaciated upland areas are valued for their landscapes and habitats, so proposals for developments need to be carefully considered to ensure they are appropriate for the area.

THE LAKE DISTRICT

An example of a glaciated upland area in the UK used for tourism

The Lake District National Park is found in the northwest of England and is well known for its stunning glaciated landscape.

Attractions for tourists

Whilst some tourists visit the Lake District to take part in adventure tourism, such as climbing Scafell Pike (highest mountain in England), others are happy to take gentle boat trips on the lakes and explore towns such as Keswick, which have many tea rooms and souvenir shops.

Strategies used to manage the impact of tourism

The 'Fix the Fells' project is tackling erosion damage to footpaths caused by severe weather events and heavy use by people. 344 upland paths are being repaired and maintained.

Section 106 agreements are used by local councils to make sure houses that are built to be affordable for local people remain so in the future.

The Lake District 2040 Vision aims to increase the number of visitors arriving by train by 50%, link the lakes together through water transport and zero carbon buses and encourage more cycling.

Social, economic and environmental impacts of tourism

Social

Low wages and high house prices in this area mean it is hard for young people to afford homes, forcing some to move away.

Economic

In 2018, 19.38 million tourists visited the Lake District, benefitting a range of businesses providing accommodation, food, drink and leisure activities.

Environmental

83% of visitors to the Lake District travel by car, leading to traffic congestion in popular spots. Tourists may park on the edge of roads, damaging the verges. However, money from tourism can also be used to conserve the area.

'The advantages of tourists visiting glaciated upland areas outweigh the disadvantages.'

Do you agree? Use an example to explain your answer. [6]

The Lake District in the north west of England is a popular tourist destination, attracting 19.38 million tourists in 2018. Tourists are attracted by the glacial scenery, including peaks and ribbon lakes. These tourists bring great economic benefits when they spend money on accommodation, food and leisure activities in towns such as Grasmere and Keswick.

The large numbers of tourists visiting popular locations such as Scafell Pike can lead to traffic congestion as 83% of visitors to the Lake District travel by car. There are plans to increase use of trains and zero carbon buses by 2040, showing that transport doesn't have to be a problem.

Money from tourism can be invested in conservation projects such as 'Fix the Fells' and legislation such as section 106 agreements can be used to make sure there is still affordable housing for people in the Lake District. This shows that, with careful management, the advantages of tourists visiting the Lake District outweigh the disadvantages.

This levels-based question should be marked in accordance with the mark bands provided on page 178.

Exam tip: Six mark questions are designed to get you thinking! This question gives a statement and asks if you agree. The best answers will include a balance of advantages and disadvantages of tourists visiting glaciated upland areas, then draw a conclusion about agreeing or disagreeing with the statement. Including an example is essential as answers with no example will be limited to level 1 marks only. Use the example throughout your answer rather than just tagging the name of a place on the end.

EXAMINATION PRACTICE

*You should study and revise **two** options from Coastal, River and Glacial landscapes in the UK.*

Coastal landscapes in the UK option

1. Explain **one** way in which material is transported at the coast. [2]

2. Look at the image of the coastline at Kilve in Somerset on **page 57**. Name one landform shown which was formed by erosional processes. [1]

3. Which **one** of these is a process which erodes cliffs along the coastline? [1]
    A. ☐ Swash
    B. ☐ Hydraulic action
    C. ☐ Longshore drift
    D. ☐ Slumping

4. Suggest **one** type of location where a spit is formed. [1]

5. Explain how sand dunes form and change over time. [4]

6. 'Hard engineering strategies are more effective in protecting coastlines than soft engineering strategies.' Do you agree? Use an example to explain your answer. [6]

River landscapes in the UK option

1. Explain **one** way in which a river's bed and banks can be eroded. [2]

2. Look at the image of heavy rainfall on **page 70**. Explain why this rainfall may lead to flooding. [1]

3. Which **one** of these processes causes the reduction in the size of material carried by a river? [1]
    A. ☐ Attrition
    B. ☐ Traction
    C. ☐ Deposition
    D. ☐ Abrasion

4. Explain why a river cliff forms on the outside of a meander. [2]

5. Explain how waterfalls form and change over time. [4]

6. 'Physical factors have a more significant influence on the shape of hydrographs than human factors.' Do you agree? [6]

Glacial landscapes in the UK option

1. Explain **one** way in which glaciers erode the landscape. [2]

2. Look at the image of scree slopes on **page 74**. State which weathering process creates scree. [1]

3. Which **one** of these landscape features is created by deposition? [1]
    A. ☐ Hanging valley
    B. ☐ Arête
    C. ☐ Drumlin
    D. ☐ Pyramidal peak

4. State what is meant by 'moraine'. [1]

5. Explain how corries form and change over time. [4]

6. Explain how conflicts can occur between people who want to use land in different ways in glaciated upland areas in the UK. [6]

Additional question

Choose **one** landscape from the figures below.

Explain how the landforms in your chosen figure are formed by physical processes. [6]

Figure 1: Coastal landscapes

Figure 2: River landscapes

Figure 3: Glacial landscapes

TOPICS FOR PAPER 2
Challenges in the human environment

Information about Paper 2

Written exam: 1 hour 30 minutes
88 marks (including 3 marks for spelling, punctuation, grammar and specialist terminology (SPaG). SPaG will only be assessed in a single extended response question where indicated).

Section A: All questions are mandatory (33 marks)
Section B: All questions are mandatory (30 marks)
Section C: Answer question 3 and any one question from 4, 5 or 6 (25 marks)
Option of Food, Water or Energy in Q4-6

35% of qualification grade

Specification coverage

Urban issues and challenges, the changing economic world and the challenge of resource management.

The content for this assessment will be drawn from the essential subject content in sections 3.2.1–3.2.3 and 3.4 of the specification.

Questions

A mix of multiple-choice, short answer and extended-writing questions assessing knowledge, understanding and skills in contextual scenarios.

URBAN ISSUES AND CHALLENGES

Urbanisation and urban trends across the world

Urbanisation occurs when the proportion of people living in urban areas in a country increases. Since 2010, more people live in urban than in rural areas across the world. Different patterns of **urban trends** can be seen in different parts of the world:

HICs

The UK and other European **higher income countries (HICs)** urbanised in the 1800s when people moved to cities following the industrial revolution. Some UK cities are now growing slowly, with the fastest growth in 2017/18 being 1.8% in Coventry, whilst the population has stabilised in others. UK cities with declining populations in 2017/18 included Oxford and Aberdeen. In 2020 83.9% of people in the UK lived in urban areas.

NEEs

Newly emerging economies (NEEs) such as South Korea, Singapore, Hong Kong and Taiwan (sometimes known as the four Asian Tigers) urbanised from the 1950s when the countries **industrialised** as part of the global shift in manufacturing. 100% of people in Singapore and Hong Kong lived in urban areas in 2020.

Some **NEEs** have industrialised recently and are still experiencing rapid urban growth. Only 15.4% of people in Nigeria lived in urban areas in 1960, but this increased to 52% by 2020.

LICs

There are very low levels of urbanisation in many **lower income countries (LICs)**. Examples include Papua New Guinea (13.5%), Burundi (14%), Sri Lanka (18.9%) and Uganda (25%). However, most LICs are now experiencing rapid urbanisation. Between 2015 and 2020 Uganda's urban population increased by 5.7%, the fastest rate in the world during this period.

Singapore

Types and effects of migration

The rate of urbanisation in a place is affected by both **migration** and **natural increase**.

Migration	**Rural-urban migration**	**Natural increase**
Movement from one place to another.	People move from the countryside to towns and cities.	Birth rate minus death rate.

National migration	**International migration**	
People move within a country.	People move from one country to another.	

Push-pull theory

In the 1960s a geographer called **Everett Lee** suggested that each place has:

Positive (or pull) factors	Negative (or push) factors
Encourage people to stay in a place or to move there.	Encourage people to move away from an area.

Whether people **migrate** or not will depend on these **push and pull factors**, potential obstacles to moving and their own personal situations. This migration may take the form of **rural-urban migration**:

People in rural areas often work in farming, fishing and mining (the primary sector) with limited opportunities to access services such as healthcare and education.

Urban areas usually provide access to a wider range of employment opportunities, services and leisure activities than rural areas.

People may be forced to leave rural areas because of conflict, natural hazards and/or changes to the climate.

> **! Note**
>
> This theory is a simple way to allow geographers to discuss migration, but it is limited as in reality people's migration stories are individual and often complex.

The emergence of megacities

A **megacity** has a population of over 10 million people. New York and Tokyo became megacities in the 1950s. This map shows the largest megacities today.

CASE STUDY LAGOS

A major city in a newly emerging economy

Lagos is a megacity in Lagos State in Nigeria. It is **located** on the Atlantic coast in the west of Nigeria (a **NEE**).

Location and importance

Lagos was the capital of Nigeria until 1991 and is the main industrial centre. In 2021 Lagos contributed over a third of the GDP of Nigeria and had the fourth highest GDP of a city in Africa.

The city is also a centre for banking in West Africa and is developing as a high-tech hub.

The Nigerian film industry, Nollywood, is the second largest in the world (after Bollywood in India and ahead of Hollywood). This is based in Lagos, which is a major centre for education and culture in Sub-Saharan Africa.

Causes of growth

Lagos had a population of nearly 15 million in 2021, an increase of 3.44% from 2020. It covers almost 1000 square kilometres. In 1950, Lagos was a coastal city with a population of only 325 000 people, but this number rapidly increased from the 1960s.

This growth is due to both **migration** and **natural increase**:

Fertility rate

The **fertility rate** in Lagos State is 3.4 children per woman, which is above the **replacement rate** of 2.1 and so leads to population growth.

Rural-urban migration

A lack of opportunities in rural Nigeria has led to high levels of **rural-urban migration** to Lagos in the last 50 years. Northern Nigeria has the highest birth rate in the world but little employment beyond farming, meaning that many young people leave to seek work in Lagos. 80% of Lagos's current growth is due to rural-urban migration.

Opportunities created by urban growth

Lagos has grown from a coastal port city to a megacity because of the opportunities it offers its residents. As the city has grown, these opportunities have multiplied due to **social** and **economic** development.

Economic development

Victoria Island is the financial centre of Lagos and also offers a wide range of shops, restaurants and entertainment venues. **Transnational Corporations** (**TNCs**) including Halliburton and IBM have offices here.

The Lekki Free Trade Zone (outside the city of Lagos in Lagos State) is a major urban industrial area which has **stimulated economic development**. It is a partnership between the Lagos State Government and a group of Chinese companies, aiming to enhance cooperation between Nigeria and China, optimise the Nigerian industrial structure and improve quality of life for Nigerians. It is hoped that over 100 000 jobs will be created, providing employment for skilled, semi-skilled and unskilled workers. A **multiplier effect** has also been created, with existing industries benefitting from new markets in the Free Trade Zone and new enterprises being developed.

The Lekki-Ikoyi bridge links the Lekki Free Trade Zone to Lagos.

Access to services and resources

Access to education	Access to water
Push	**Push**
Primary education is free in Nigeria, but in the rural north of the country only 43% of children attend school because of poverty, cultural barriers and a lack of access to schools in remote areas. Conflict in north eastern Nigeria means 802 schools have closed.	The north of Nigeria is dry and often suffers from droughts, causing **water insecurity**. Militants have sometimes poisoned water sources as part of the conflict. Water quality has been affected by oil spills in the Niger Delta region.
Pull	**Pull**
Wealthy people in Lagos send their children to private international schools. Whilst other children attend schools which are often underfunded, Nigerians recognise the importance of education in development and tackling poverty. Cities often provide better schools than the countryside. The University of Lagos claims to be 'the university of first choice and the nation's pride'.	The Lagos Water Corporation say they provide *"safe drinking water in sufficient and regular quality to over 12.5 million people."* However, the poorest face water insecurity.

Access to healthcare

Push

Conflict has also affected healthcare in the northeast of Nigeria. Some health centres have been destroyed and others are struggling to cope as people have moved to safer regions. 46% of health facilities have been destroyed or damaged in Borno, Adamawa and Yobe states.

Pull

The Lagos State Health Scheme (LSHS) aims to register all residents of the city and state of Lagos so that they can get compulsory health insurance and therefore access to basic healthcare. 40 000 people have been provided with free health insurance. There are far more doctors and nurses in Lagos than in rural areas and roughly 300 primary health care centres.

Access to electricity

Push

Nearly 45% of Nigeria was without electricity in 2018. It is difficult to connect remote rural areas to the Nigerian Energy Grid. There has been a lack of investment in stand alone schemes and a lack of skilled people to design and carry out projects.

Pull

96% of households in Lagos had access to electricity in 1997. The Lagos Energy Market was announced in 2021, aiming to improve the city and state's energy supplies separately from the Nigerian Energy Grid and use more sustainable sources.

Challenges created by urban growth

Managing urban growth

Urban growth has put pressure on housing in Lagos, with the population density increasing to 209 people per hectare. (New York has 25.) 60% of people can't afford good quality housing, so they live in settlements which are sometimes labelled as **slums** or **squatter settlements**. This housing is often poor quality, there is a lack of **infrastructure** and people face insecurity as they could be evicted at any time.

People work hard to improve the quality of life in their communities. The Nigerian Slum/Informal Settlement Federation is a movement created by the **urban poor** in Nigeria. They have set up community based savings groups and have collected data to create maps which can be used to identity needs and plan solutions.

Mokoko in Lagos is one of the areas labelled a slum. It has its own character and issues alongside its difficulties

Energy

Most households have access to electricity in Lagos, but in slums this might only be for part of the day and is likely to come from polluting generators.

JEI Nigeria is an **NGO (non-governmental organisation)** working in Lagos. Their para-legal team works with people so that they know their rights and can fight for **access to services** and against police brutality and eviction. They also run workshops to teach local people how to build solar panels and streetlamps.

Access to healthcare and education services

Health in 'slums' is poor due to the combination of low quality housing, **contaminated water** and overcrowding. People suffer infectious diseases such as TB, hepatitis, dengue and cholera, but are also at a high risk of asthma, heart problems, diabetes and mental health problems. Free access to the Lagos State Health Scheme (LSHS) is tackling this, but many are still to register.

Children in Lagos have access to a free education, but the government and low cost private schools in the 'slum' areas are often poor quality. Class sizes are large, there is a lack of facilities such as toilets and quality of teaching varies greatly. **Poverty** means children may not be able to go to school as they need to work to support their families, or they may not be able to afford uniform and equipment. One solution is for companies to sponsor schools, another is for NGOs to provide support. Nigeria's government will need to take action if it is to achieve **Sustainable Development Goal 4** and provide 'Quality Education for All'.

Clean water and sanitation systems

People in slums often lack access to clean water, so new boreholes have been drilled and **sanitation** improved (by using composting toilets). Sea level rise due to **climate change** is also a threat to water supplies and homes in these coastal communities.

Reducing unemployment and crime

65% of Lagosians work in the **informal sector**, doing jobs such as driving taxis, cleaning and selling goods. These jobs are insecure and many people suffered extreme poverty when the COVID pandemic meant they couldn't work. Lagos also suffers from **crime**, including bribery and corruption, drugs trade, property crimes and violent crime. CCTV cameras have been installed around the city to monitor and tackle crime and many areas have set up Neighbourhood Safety Corps.

Managing environmental issues

Air pollution

Air pollution is a particular problem in Lagos. The World Bank estimates that in 2018, air pollution caused the city losses of $2.1 billion and 11,200 premature deaths. Most of the emissions come from road traffic.

Traffic congestion

Lagos suffers from **traffic congestion**, which has not been significantly reduced despite a Bus Rapid Transit system being built in 2008. The World Bank is supporting initiatives to improve public transport in Lagos.

Waste disposal

The **waste disposal system** in Lagos was set up in the 1970s when the population was 3 million – it struggles to cope with the waste from 20 million today. There is a huge dumpsite at Olusoson and some people dump and burn their own waste. The 'Clean Lagos' initiative has been introduced to tackle this and rules for sulphur content in fuels have been tightened up to reduce air pollution.

LAGOS RENT-TO-OWN STRATEGY

An example of how urban planning is improving the quality of life for the urban poor

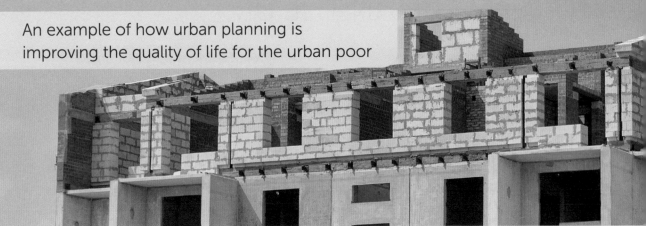

Rent-To-Own is an affordable housing policy by the Lagos State Government.

Mission

To ensure the provision of adequate and good quality housing in Lagos Mega City and facilitate easy access of its citizens to home ownership.

Rent-To-Own

This scheme was launched by the Lagos State Government in 2016. People who want to own a home pay 5% of its value, then move in, paying the rest of the cost as rent towards the ownership of the property over 10 years.

5008 housing units were initially made available in 12 housing estates across the city, with plans to provide 20 000 more in five years.

This scheme has provided the urban poor with access to affordable good quality housing. Many Lagosians spend over 50% of their income on rent, so affordable housing payments mean they have more disposable income to spend on food, healthcare and more, improving their quality of life. Good quality housing also means people are more likely to be healthy.

Using an example, explain how an urban planning strategy can improve quality of life for the urban poor.
[6]

Around 60% of people in Lagos live in unsatisfactory housing, which affects their health and wellbeing. The Lagos Rent to Own Strategy allows people to pay 5% of the cost of a home, then pay the rest off over the next 10 years. The homes are connected to water, sanitation and electricity systems, reducing likelihood of residents suffering from infectious diseases such as typhoid. Having a secure, affordable home also supports good mental health for the urban poor, so improving their quality of life. This levels-based question should be marked in accordance with the mark bands provided on page 178.

POPULATION DISTRIBUTION AND MAJOR CITIES IN THE UK

Population density

Population density is the number of people living in each square kilometre in an area. As the **choropleth map** below shows, population density varies greatly across the UK, with **dense** populations found in the South East and the Midlands and **sparse** populations in areas such as the highlands of Scotland.

Development of major cities

The major cities in the UK developed as the country industrialised. Some were administration centres, others were ports and/or areas of manufacturing. Industrial cities initially grew up near sources of raw materials such as coal and iron ore.

5000+ people / Km²
2500–5000
1000–2499
500–999
250–499
100–249
50–99
25–49
0–24

Using the map above, describe the distribution of major cities across the UK. [2]

Most cities are located in the centre of the UK, including Birmingham, Sheffield and Manchester.[1] Cities not in this cluster are on or near the coast, such as Bristol, Cardiff and Belfast.[1]

CASE STUDY BRISTOL

A major city in the UK

Location and importance

Bristol is a city in the west of England. It is located on the River Avon.

Bristol is a well connected city, with the M5 motorway to the west, the M4 to the north and the M32 leading into the city centre. Temple Meads railway station is a transport hub for the city and Bristol International Airport is to the south west of the city.

This city is important in the UK as it is a centre for aerospace, technology, banking and insurance. There are two universities, the University of Bristol and the University of the West of England (UWE).

Bristol developed as a port and played an important role in world trade. Bristol was the leading slaving port in the UK in the late 1730s and many of the factories that developed in the city at this time processed goods such as cotton and sugar obtained through enslaved labour. When the slave trade ended, slave owners received compensation for their losses, leading to a boom in investment in Bristol and new building works. Bristol harbour is now used for leisure and tourism in the city centre, whilst the port of Avonmouth and Royal Portbury Docks still play a role in global trade. Bristol is the seventh most popular city for international tourists in the UK.

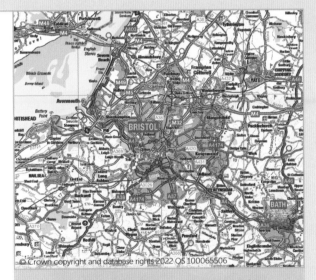

© Crown copyright and database rights 2022 OS 100065506

Georgian buildings such as those in Queen Square were often homes to merchants who benefitted from slavery.

Impacts of national and international migration

Bristol was heavily bombed in WWII and the population of the city declined after the war, stabilising in the 1990s. The city saw rapid growth from 2000 to 2010 and is still growing slowly. The city council estimated that the population of Bristol was 463 400 in 2020, reflecting an increase of 11.7% since 2008.

↑	**Natural increase**	2017/18 = 5 900 births − 3 500 deaths = 2 400
↓	**Net national migration**	2017/18 = 34 700 in - 35 100 out = − 400
↑	**Net international migration**	2017/18 = 7 500 in − 5 400 out = 2 100

People have moved from London and the South East of England to Bristol as house prices and the costs of living are lower. The most common places of birth for migrants born outside of the UK are Poland, Somalia, India and Jamaica. These last three countries were part of the **British Empire**, so their people were British citizens until the countries declared independence. Many Polish people joined the British armed forces during the Second World War and settled in the UK after the war because their country was under a communist government.

Bristol celebrates its **multicultural population** with events such as the St Paul's Carnival. Whilst many Bristolians enjoy how the city has changed due to **cultural mixing**, there are concerns that house prices have been forced up by national migration from the South East and developments of luxury apartments are unaffordable for locals. There are also concerns about the 'studentification' of some parts of Bristol as old buildings are replaced with accommodation blocks. (There were 54 000 students registered at Bristol's two universities in 2017/18.)

Bristol is also reflecting on its past and making changes. An example is that Colston Girls' School changed its name to Montpelier High School in 2021 to end its connection with the slave trader.

Opportunities created by urban change

Social and economic opportunities

Cultural mix

Bristol is culturally diverse with people from 187 different countries.

Employment

The **employment rate** in Bristol in 2021 was 77.1%, the second highest in the UK. The sectors employing the most people at this time were health and social work (15.2 %), professional, scientific and technical activities (12.8%) and wholesale and retail trade (11.7%). Bristol is a popular locational choice for transnational corporations (TNCs) such as Airbus, BT, Dyson and IBM.

Recreation and entertainment

Harbourside **regeneration** has created a hub for entertainment, dining and leisure, including the M-Shed and the SS Great Britain. Close by Millennium Square is home to the 'We The Curious' science exploration centre and the Aquarium.

Transport

Bristol's integrated transport system (ITS) has been developed around the hub of Temple Meads Station. The rail station building was regenerated in 2021 and the line to London electrified. Metrobuses run around the city and there are water taxis connecting the station, the harbourside and the shopping centre at Broadmead.

Environmental opportunities

Urban greening

In 2015 Bristol became the first city in the UK to be a European Green Capital. The city has over 400 parks and gardens. The Avon Wildlife Trust manages over 1100 hectares of Nature Reserve sites in and around Bristol.

Social and economic challenges

Decline of industry

Bristol's city centre port closed in 1977.

Many industries in the city centre declined as a result of the port closure and pockets of **urban deprivation** developed.

Housing developments

There are also inequalities between areas because of the way they developed. Before 1919, housing was built by **private developers**. Following the 1919 Housing and Town Planning Act, housing estates were built in places such as Knowle. This **social housing** was good quality and anyone who could afford the rent could live there. Bristol was heavily bombed during WWII, so temporary prefabricated homes known as **prefabs** were built in places including Avonmouth. More council estates were developed after the war and **tower blocks** such as Canynge House were built on bombsites in the inner city.

By the 1980s, some of the estates had fallen into decline and building homes in tower blocks was seen as a mistake. Prefabs ended up as permanent housing even though they had never been designed for this. There are clear **inequalities** in housing, education, health and employment across Bristol, as can be seen by comparing two areas, or **wards**:

2020/21 statistics (unless otherwise stated)	Filwood	Clifton	Bristol average
Crime (per 1000 people)	126.2	51.2	101
GCSE attainment score (2018)	34	51.8	44.2
Social housing %	41.3	9.1	20.3
% who say they are in good health	77	88	87
Male life expectancy (years)	76.2	82.2	78.5
% aged 16–74 economically active (2011)	62.9	69.9	70.6

 Note

Care needs to be taken to avoid constructing a single view of an area from these statistics. Filwood Green Business Park opened in 2015. There is a thriving community centre and green spaces are well maintained and used.

Challenges created by urban change continued

Environmental challenges

Dereliction

When industries declined in Bristol city centre in the 1980s some buildings fell derelict. The cinema in Filwood closed in the 1990s and remained derelict in 2021.

Building on greenfield sites

Greenfield sites haven't been built on before. The people of South Bristol protested when a development was proposed for Novers Hill, a green area near Filwood. They were concerned about habitat loss and over development.

Waste disposal

Bristol identified disposal of food waste as a particular problem, with 20 000 tonnes of food waste put in black bins each year. The #SlimMyWaste campaign provided education on cutting food waste and disposing of it in designated food bins.

Building on brownfield sites

Derelict buildings have been cleared in parts of Bristol to make way for new ones. An example is the old Post Office depot which was demolished to make way for University of Bristol's new Temple Quarter Enterprise Campus.

Urban sprawl and commuter settlements

Urban sprawl on the rural-urban fringe

Some greenfield developments can cause the city to spread into the countryside, which is known as **urban sprawl**. The rural-urban fringe is the edge of the city.

Growth of commuter settlements

Counter urbanisation happens when people leave cities to live in the countryside, often **commuting** (travelling) to work in the city. Settlements such as Nailsea and Yatton have grown rapidly since the 1980s, including development of large **greenfield sites**.

TEMPLE QUARTER ENTERPRISE ZONE

Example of an urban regeneration project

The development of Bristol's Temple Quarter is one of the UK's largest urban regeneration projects.

Mission
"We are aiming to create a sustainable and flourishing new urban quarter for Bristol: a place that is welcoming to all – to live, work, study, enjoy leisure time and build on Bristol's strengths as a world class city." **– Marvin Rees, Mayor of Bristol**

Enterprise zone

Enterprise Zones are areas designated by the government for regeneration and development. Businesses are offered **incentives** such as reduced business rates to locate in these Zones. The Temple Quarter Enterprise Zone was launched in 2012, covering an area of 130 hectares around Bristol Temple Meads Station.

This area was in need of **regeneration** as it had fallen into decline in the 1980s following the closure of the port. **Deindustrialisation** saw industries moving overseas as part of the global shift, leaving **derelict** buildings and unemployment.

This 25 year regeneration project aims to develop **brownfield sites** to create a 'thriving, well-connected, mixed-use community'. The aim is to create 10 000 new homes, 22 000 new jobs and bring £1.6bn annual income to Bristol.

Key developments

The regeneration project combines repurposing old buildings and clearing areas for new buildings. There is also an emphasis on improved **infrastructure**, with superfast broadband and improved vehicle, cycle and pedestrian access.

The Engine Shed in Temple Quarter Enterprise Zone

The **Engine Shed** is a Grade 1 listed building next to Bristol Temple Meads which has become an Enterprise Hub. £1.7 million was invested to create business spaces, Brunel's Boardroom meeting suite and event spaces. Companies based there in 2021 included Boomsatsuma and TechSPARK. Engine Shed has close links to the University of Bristol, which is also leading the development of the **Temple Quarter Enterprise Campus**. This is an example of a **derelict** building (brownfield site) being cleared to make way for a new £300 million campus.

To what extent has urban change been successful in tackling social and economic challenges?   [9]

Temple Quarter Enterprise Zone in Bristol was launched in 2012 to bring investment to the area around Bristol Temple Meads station, which had fallen into decline. The area was suffering from urban deprivation, affecting the quality of life of people who lived there due to unemployment and a lack of opportunities.

The aim is to create a mixed-use development including 10 000 new homes and 22 000 jobs. There is an emphasis on infrastructure, with superfast broadband and an integrated transport system. A sense of community is being developed by encouraging people to live, work and socialise in the inner city rather than commuting in from outside. Being well connected and having a strong sense of community is helping to tackle social challenges in the area.

The Engine Shed has been regenerated to create a high-tech hub in a listed building. This is led by the University of Bristol, who are also developing a Temple Quarter Enterprise Campus to cater for 3500 students and provide training and skills centre for use by community groups. These facilities tackle economic challenges in the area by providing jobs and giving local people the chance to gain new skills, improving their employability.

However, it is important to question how much people who already live in this area will benefit. They may not be able to afford the new homes and may not have the right skills to get jobs in the new high-tech businesses. This could cause social exclusion, with local people feeling pushed out by new arrivals. I therefore think that this regeneration project has been successful to some extent in tackling social and economic challenges, but not fully successful.

This levels-based question should be marked in accordance with the mark bands provided on page 179.

URBAN SUSTAINABILITY

Definition

AQA defines a sustainable city as:

"one in which there is minimal damage to the environment, the economic base is sound with resources allocated fairly and jobs secure, and there is a strong sense of community, with local people involved in decisions made. Sustainable urban living includes several aims including the use of renewable resources, energy efficiency, use of public transport, accessible resources and services."

Having previously studied Bristol as a case study of a UK city – you can also use the city to illustrate how urban areas can become more sustainable.

Water and energy conservation

Sustainable cities aspire to minimise the use of water whilst maximising supplies. This can involve efficient collection of water, **recycling** water and **conserving groundwater supplies**.

One way Bristol is conserving water is using a wild rainwater streets approach. This involves planting trees (urban greening), use of permeable paving and encouraging residents to use water butts to collect water to use in their gardens.

Energy conservation involves saving energy, using technology to improve energy efficiency and **developing renewable energy**.

The Warmer Homes, Advice and Money (WHAM) project in Bristol brings organisations including the council, Citizens Advice and Bristol Energy Network together to support low income families to access grants and install energy saving measures such as draught proofing and insulation.

Waste recycling

Bristol is minimising waste sent for disposal and is recycling more waste using kerb side collections and education campaigns. Food waste and human waste is used to power Bristol's bio 'poo buses' as part of its integrated transport system. This approach reduces pollution and the need to extract new raw materials.

Creating green space

Over a third of Bristol is open space, including parks and public gardens. Bristol is keen to:

- Protect green spaces and improve their quality
- Make green spaces more accessible to people
- Create new green spaces

Bristol's Parks and Green Spaces Strategy has these goals at its heart, as well as protecting green spaces from development and encouraging local people to be involved in improving the green spaces in their area.

Cabot Tower in Brandon Park

Urban transport strategies

Integrated transport systems (ITS) aim to tackle traffic congestion, making transport more efficient and reducing air pollution.

Bristol's ITS is centred on Bristol Temple Meads, with three bus routes linking the station to the main entertainment and shopping areas and to Park and Ride sites. Cycling and walking are encouraged, with new paths and improved facilities for storing bicycles at Temple Meads and in other locations.

Cycle storage at Bristol Temple Meads station

Suggest how introducing urban traffic strategies can make cities more sustainable. [4]

Traffic can harm the environment in cities as new roads and car parks increase impermeable surfaces and exhaust fumes cause air pollution. Traffic congestion can affect the sustainability of the city's economy as workers and deliveries face delays. Developing integrated transport schemes such as the one centred around Bristol's Temple Meads station means more people use public transport and cycle, reducing the need for new roads and air pollution whilst also supporting the economy.

This levels-based question should be marked in accordance with the mark bands provided on page 178.

EXAMINATION PRACTICE

1. Which of these statements defines the term national migration? [1]

    A. ☐ People moving from one country to another

    B. ☐ People commuting to work in a nearby town

    C. ☐ People moving from one part of a country to another part of the same country

    D. ☐ Any movement of people from one place to another

2. Study the figure, which shows the percentage of urban and rural populations in Turkey (NEE) between 1927 and 2012.

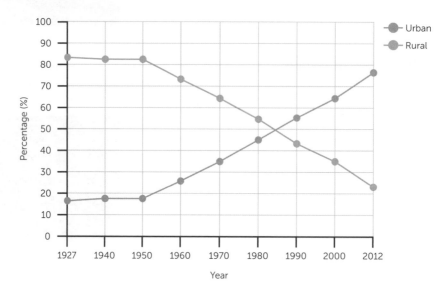

    Complete the paragraph to describe the changes shown **in the figure**. Choose **three** correct answers from this list: [3]

    great   **urbanisation**   **little**   **1990**   **1980**   **regeneration**

    Between 1927 and 1950 there was _____ change in the percentage of people living in rural and urban areas in Turkey. In 1950 the process of _____ started, with an increasing proportion of people moving to cities. The number of people living in urban areas was greater than the number of people living in rural areas in Turkey in _____.

3. Study the extract from a news article below, which considers the situation in Yemen (LIC) in 2021.

    In 2015, ongoing conflict in the Yemen reached a point at which it was cited as the worst humanitarian crisis the world had seen. Fighting resulted in 110,000 fatalities sparking severe malnutrition of half of children under five years old and over 12 million others reliant on food aid.

    Using information from the extract, suggest **two** reasons why migrants are leaving Yemen. [2]

4. Study the figure below, a photograph showing traffic congestion in London.

Using the photograph, suggest **one** way in which traffic congestion could cause problems for London's economy. [2]

5. Using the photograph above and a case study of a city in the UK, assess the environmental challenges that can be created by urban change. [6]

6. Look at the table of statistics comparing Filwood and Clifton in Bristol (also on **page 96**).

2020/21 statistics (unless otherwise stated)	Filwood	Clifton	Bristol average
Crime (per 1000 people)	126.2	51.2	101
GCSE attainment score (2018)	34	51.8	44.2
Social housing %	41.3	9.1	20.3
% who say they are in good health	77	88	87
Male life expectancy (years)	76.2	82.2	78.5
% 16–74 yrs economically active (2011)	62.9	69.9	70.6

(a) Calculate the percentage increase in the level of crime between Clifton and Filwood to one decimal place. [1]

(b) Using information from the table and your own knowledge, suggest reasons for inequalities in housing, health and employment across Bristol. [4]

7. Outline **one** pull factor that may encourage people in LICs or NEEs to move to cities from rural areas. [2]

8. To what extent has urban growth brought challenges to a city in a LIC or a NEE that you have studied? [9 + 3 SPAG]

THE CHANGING ECONOMIC WORLD

Organisations attempt to classify different parts of the world into different categories of development.

Global variations in economic development and quality of life

The World Bank classifies countries according to their **Gross National Income** (GNI) **per capita**:

Low-income economies	$1,035 or less in 2020
Lower-middle income economies	$1,036 to $4,045
Upper-middle income economies	$4,046 to $12,535
High-income economies	$12,536 or more

GCSE Geography considers both **higher income** and **lower income countries**. It also includes a classification of **Newly Emerging Economies (NEEs)**.

AQA defines NEEs as *"Countries that have begun to experience higher rates of economic development, usually with higher levels of industrialisation. They differ from LICs in that they no longer rely primarily on agriculture, have made gains in infrastructure and industrial growth, and are experiencing increasing incomes and high levels of investment, e.g. Brazil, Russia, China and South Africa (the so-called BRICS countries)."*

This classification considers **economic development**, but it is also important to think about quality of life in different places. Some countries are wealthy but don't share the benefits of this wealth across their population, leading to **inequalities**. This is why it is also important to look at **social indicators**.

Economic and social measures of development

Gross National Income (GNI) per head/capita

GNI includes the value of goods and services in an area and also income from investments overseas. GNI per head is GNI divided by the number of people in the area.

Infant mortality rate

Average number of deaths of children under 1 year old per 1000 live births in a year.

Birth and death rates

Births/deaths per 1000 people in a year.

People per doctor

The number of people in a place divided by the number of doctors.

Life expectancy

The average number of years a person might be expected to live.

Human Development Index (HDI) (See **page 106**.)

An index created using GDP (Gross Domestic Product) per capita, life expectancy and adult literacy/years in school.

Access to safe water

% of people who can access enough clean water.

Literacy rate

Adults able to read and write.

Limitations of economic and social measures

Using only one indicator gives a limited view of development in a place. Using a range of social and economic indicators, or an index such as the **HDI**, gives a fuller picture. However, there are still limitations as indicators are averages for an area, so they cover up differences between different places within the area or different groups of people. Some people also criticise the focus on economic growth as this may harm the environment.

The Demographic Transition Model (DTM) and development

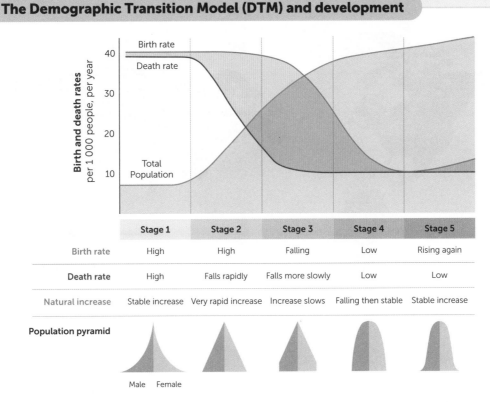

The DTM shows how population changes as a place moves through different stages of development. It shows how **birth and death rates** change and resulting changes in the **natural increase**.

Look at the diagram showing the DTM on this page. Describe how natural increase changes as a country becomes more developed.

[3]

At Stage 1 a country is at a low level of development and the population isn't increasing.[1] As it moves into Stages 2 to 4 there is a large difference between the birth rate and death rate so there is rapid natural increase.[1] By Stage 5, the country is highly developed, and the natural increase stabilises.[1]

CAUSES OF UNEVEN DEVELOPMENT

Uneven development

The map below shows the **Human Development Index** (**HDI**) for the countries of the world, highlighting how uneven levels of development are. Reasons for **uneven development** are complex, but three major factors are physical geography, the economic situation and the historical background of countries.

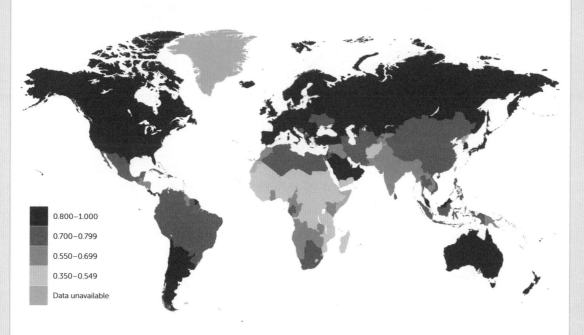

0.800–1.000

0.700–0.799

0.550–0.699

0.350–0.549

Data unavailable

Physical causes

Trade may be limited if a country is **landlocked** (no coastline) or has a barrier such as a **mountain range** separating it from other countries. However, a mountain range could also create tourism opportunities. **Navigable rivers** (suitable for boats) can benefit trade. **Extreme environments** (e.g. deserts, rainforests or tundra) can limit development.

Economic causes

Countries in **trading blocs** such as the European Union or the North American Free Trade Agreement benefit from free trade across the bloc which can help countries develop. The global shift in the economy means **TNCs** now have operations in different parts of the world, which can affect levels of development.

Historical causes

During colonial times, **imperial powers** became very wealthy by extracting resources and labour from **colonies**. Past **conflict** has also affected the development of countries.

CONSEQUENCES OF UNEVEN DEVELOPMENT ON WEALTH AND HEALTH

Uneven development has serious **consequences** for the world. People suffer from poor **quality of life** if they are trapped in **poverty**, but **inequalities** also have global consequences when it comes to tackling challenges such as pandemics.

Disparities in health

- Countries with a higher GNI per head can use **taxes** to fund a **health service** for their populations, whilst individuals can afford a healthy diet and access to exercise through gyms and sport.

- People in HICs often die of **chronic diseases** such as cancer and heart disease as the populations are **ageing**.

- The USA is an **anomaly**. It spends more money on healthcare per person than any other country, but the **life expectancy** is lower than in many other HICs. This is because of the way healthcare is organised and the choices people make for their diet and lifestyle.

- Cuba is also an **anomaly**. It has a **GNI per head** of $8630 but the government has prioritised healthcare, so the system is one of the best in the world with **life expectancy** the same as in the USA.

- **Infectious diseases** such as malaria, diarrhoea and TB cause far more deaths in LICs than in HICs.

Disparities in wealth

- In 2020, Switzerland (HIC) had a **Gross National Income (GNI) per head** of $82 620 in comparison to $230 in Burundi (LIC).

- In 2019, the fastest growing economy was the USA, but the economies of Venezuela, Iran and Zimbabwe shrank.

CONSEQUENCES OF UNEVEN DEVELOPMENT FOR INTERNATIONAL MIGRATION

Uneven development can lead to international migration as people move to more developed countries to improve their **quality of life**.

Movement of people

The UK has experienced several waves of international migration. People from **colonies** had citizen status and were encouraged to move to the UK to fill labour shortages after WWII. Migrants from the Caribbean became known as 'the Windrush generation'

European countries are in discussion about how to cope with migration across the Mediterranean from North Africa. Between January and September 2021 there were 80 680 attempted crossings. 22 930 migrants were recorded as dead or missing in the Mediterranean Sea between 2014 and 2021, causing families and friends to suffer.

The UK introduced the 'hostile environment' approach to migration in 2012, making it difficult for people to stay in the UK if they didn't have 'leave to return' and being less welcoming to new migrants.

Table showing development indicators for different countries (2020 data)

Country	GNI per head ($)	Doctors per 1000 people	Life expectancy (years)
USA	64 550	2.6	79.11
Sweden	54 050	4.3	83.33
UK	39 700	5.8	81.77
Cuba	8 630	8.4	79.18
Botswana	6 640	0.3	69.86
Burundi	230	0.1	62.71

Using the table above, describe the relationship between level of development and health in the countries shown. [4]

Countries with higher GNI per head generally have higher life expectancies, suggesting a positive relationship between development and health. However, the USA has the highest GNI per capita of all the countries in the table, but the fourth highest life expectancy and only 2.6 doctors per 1000 people. Cuba has the fourth highest GNI per head but the highest number of doctors per 1000 people and a higher life expectancy than the USA. See levels-based mark scheme on page 178.

REDUCING THE GLOBAL DEVELOPMENT GAP

Development is uneven across the world. There are a range of strategies that aim to reduce this global development gap.

Strategies to reduce the global development gap

Investment

Many LICs have a negative **balance of trade** – they are spending more on imports than they are earning from exports. This is often because they sell **primary products** such as sugar and coffee. Investment in agro-processing and manufacturing industries can help countries earn more from exports and so close the development gap.

Chinese companies are working with the Lagos State Government to develop the Lekki Free Trade Zone (see **page 87**). This is just one of 25 economic and trade cooperation zones created by China in 16 African countries by the end of 2020, with a total **investment** of $735 billion. China became the African continent's most important trading partner in 2009 and more than a million Chinese workers have moved to countries in Africa.

Industrial development and tourism

Investment in industries can provide a **multiplier effect**, with suppliers and retailers benefitting from new developments. However, there can also be problems with **corruption** and **leakage** (money sent back to the home countries of TNCs and not spent locally).

Growing links between African countries and China have also brought benefits in terms of **tourism**. Countries such as Morocco, Madagascar, Namibia and South Africa have been marketing holidays during Golden Week and Chinese New Year, when many Chinese look to travel. They have also reduced visa requirements. Morocco hopes that attracting tourists from new markets will bring an additional one million jobs and boost the contribution of tourism to GNI, narrowing the development gap.

FURTHER STRATEGIES TO REDUCE THE GLOBAL DEVELOPMENT GAP

Aid

Money, goods, technology and expertise may be provided to help through:

Bilateral aid

Provided by one government to another (often with conditions attached to make sure both countries benefit).

Multilateral aid

From organisations such as the World Bank (who may also include conditions).

World Bank

NGOs

Aid from **Non Governmental Organisations (NGOs)** such as charities: Often smaller scale but with fewer conditions.

Short term aid

Often emergency aid in response to a crisis.

Long term aid

Includes rebuilding after a disaster and improving education.

Criticism of aid projects

Some aid projects have been criticised for being wasteful or going to countries that could afford to help their own populations. **Environmental damage** caused by past aid projects such as the Volta Dam in Ghana has now been recognised. Some people think it would be more appropriate to pay **reparations** to countries harmed by the transatlantic slave trade and colonialism rather than giving aid.

Aid can reduce the development gap by improving people's quality of life by improving job opportunities and access to services.

Refer back to **pages 6–10** to see the examples of short and long term aid provided in the event of natural hazards.

Intermediate technology

This **sustainable** approach involves using low cost, repairable technology instead of high cost technology that only specialists can use and repair. The NGO Practical Action is working with farmers in Senegal to build **micro-hydro systems** so that they can generate sustainable energy to help them farm more efficiently.

Fairtrade

Fairtrade products don't just mean better prices and working conditions for farm workers, they also involve a Fairtrade Premium which is spent on community projects such as education or healthcare. The development gap is therefore narrowed by workers having more money to improve their homes and diets, for example, but also through improved facilities which mean children will grow up more healthily and with a higher level of education.

However, Fairtrade goods often cost more, so only wealthier consumers can afford them.

Debt relief

The **debt crisis** in the 1980s came about because many LICs borrowed money from the World Bank to develop, then they found that they couldn't afford to make repayments when the interest rates increased. The G8 (a group of eight of the wealthiest countries in the world) voted in 2005 to cancel some of the debts of **highly indebted poor countries (HIPCs)** as long as they met certain conditions. 36 HIPCs had their debts to the International Monetary Fund (IMF) cancelled by 2015, saving US$75 billion. This meant that they could spend more money on education and health care, narrowing the development gap.

Microfinance loans

Many people across the world who live in poverty have no access to bank accounts or loans. Giving them access to small loans, or **microfinance**, means they can invest in business opportunities to earn more money and improve their quality of life.

Explain how microfinance can reduce the development gap. [4]

An example of microfinance is the Grameen Bank in Bangladesh, which loans small amounts of money to marginalised people which they pay back with a little interest. People can invest this money in a business opportunity such as making food, using their profit to pay back the loan, with money left over benefitting their family. This may mean they can send their children to school or afford medicine, improving quality of life and so reducing the development gap. See mark scheme on page 178.

RWANDA

An example of how the growth of tourism helps to reduce the development gap in a LIC

Rwanda has four national parks, six volcanoes, 23 lakes and several rare species including mountain gorillas to attract tourists. In the last decade, it has marketed itself as a place to hold conferences and events.

Tourism in Rwanda

Tourism contributed 15.1% to Rwanda's **Gross Domestic Product (GDP)** in 2019, a large increase from 4.7% in 2000. Tourism **revenues** totalled $498 million in 2019, with over 1.63 million visitors coming to the country. 90 000 jobs have been created by tourism (13% of employment in the country).

Rwanda has built a world class conference centre in Kigali and successfully attracted **TNCs** including Marriott, Radisson and Sheraton to build hotels there. The visa process has been moved online making it easier for tourists to apply to visit and the national airline, RwandAir, saw rapid growth.

Tourism has helped reduce the development gap in Rwanda by encouraging **investment**, providing employment and increasing the GDP. It can cause a **multiplier effect** i.e. by wages from tourism being spent in other businesses and by local businesses supplying goods to TNCs.

Rwanda was forced to close its borders to passenger flights on March 20th 2020 because of the COVID 19 pandemic, which had a massive impact on the tourist industry.

CASE STUDY NIGERIA

Rapid economic development of a NEE

Some LICs and NEEs are experiencing rapid economic development which leads to significant social, environmental and cultural change.

See **page 86** for examples of how aspects of Nigerian culture such as Nollywood have spread around the world.

Location and importance of Nigeria, regionally and globally

Nigeria is a NEE, located in West Africa and bordered by Niger, Chad, Cameroon and Benin. Its coastline is on the Atlantic Ocean.

The country is important in West Africa as it is the largest economy and often takes leadership roles, for example in forming the African Union.

Nigeria is important globally through its role in world trade, and in 2021 Nigerian economist Ngozi Okonjo-Iweala became the first woman and the first African to lead the World Trade Organisation.

The Nigerian diaspora (spread of people) is also important globally, with 1.24 million Nigerians living in other countries.

The main areas of Nigeria

250 minority groups make up a third of Nigeria's population, each with their own languages and traditions.

North ✳

Mainly **Hausa-Fulani** people live in this area and are Muslim. There is **desert** in the north and **grassland** in the south. About half of Nigeria's population live here.

South West ✳

Yoruba people live in this area. It is the most developed area, including Lagos. It is hot and wet with **forests**.

South East ✳

Igbo people come from this area, but many have migrated as it has few resources. This area is hot, wet and **forested**.

In 1884, representatives of 14 European powers divided Africa up between them at the Berlin Conference. No Africans were present. This is how Nigeria was created, as a **British colony**. Britain and Nigeria remain linked through the **Commonwealth**.

Britain had already developed a relationship with Nigeria, trafficking slaves from Lagos between 1790 and 1807, then developing a trade in palm oil from 1815 to 1840, introducing the process of growing **cash crops**. The **infrastructure** of Nigeria was developed to allow more trade inland, but forced labour was sometimes used.

Nigeria celebrated **independence** in 1960, but a military coup took place in 1966 and a group of army officers took control of the country. A two-and-a-half-year civil war was triggered by the declaration of an independent state of Biafra in 1967, causing mass migration, 100 000 military casualties and 2 million people in need of food aid to prevent starvation. In 1979 the military lost power. The 1970s also saw an oil boom in Nigeria.

More recently, elections in 2011 and 2015 have been declared free and fair, leading to increased political stability in the country. Nigeria has attracted **investment** from **TNCs** and transformed from being a **LIC** to a **NEE**.

Transnational Corporations (TNCs) in Nigeria

The Shell Petroleum Development Company (SPDC) of Nigeria produces 39% of Nigeria's oil and is based in the Niger Delta. This company is a joint venture between the Nigerian National Petroleum Corporation and Shell. Shell plc is a Transnational Corporation which has extracted oil in Nigeria since 1956.

Advantages	Disadvantages
SPDC employs 4500 people directly (95% are Nigerian) and 20 000 people indirectly. Investment in infrastructure, such as roads, has not only helped the oil industry, it has also benefited local people. Shell paid the Nigerian government $3.2 billion in taxes, royalties and fees in 2020.	Oil spills have polluted water and soil in the delta over the past 60+ years, affecting habitats, farming and fishing. In 2021, Shell was ordered to pay $111 million compensation to a community affected by an oil spill in the 1960s.

The changing industrial structure in Nigeria

The balance between different sectors of the economy

Study the triangle graph shown. Most of Nigeria's GDP came from the **primary sector** (accessing raw materials e.g. farming) in 1975. By 2014, the **tertiary sector** (services) contributed most to GDP and this was still the case in 2020. The **secondary sector** (manufacturing) has seen a gradual rise in share of GDP over the period.

Share of Nigeria's GDP

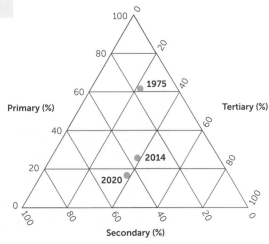

Primary (%)

Tertiary (%)

Secondary (%)

1975

2014

2020

Stimulating economic development through manufacturing

Cash crops such as palm oil (see **page 114**) were established in Nigeria in the 1800s. Crude oil was extracted in the Niger Delta from the 1930s, also contributing to the primary sector's past dominance of GDP. There was some investment in secondary industries when Nigeria was a colony and following independence, but **conflict** in the 1980s discouraged investment for a while. Political stability since 2011 has led to more foreign investment and there has been rapid growth in tertiary industries such as banking and retail. In 2011, Nigeria was included with Mexico, Indonesia and Turkey as **MINT countries**, with fast growing economies suitable for investment.

The Nigerian government has been keen to attract investment into manufacturing industries as processed goods sell for more money, helping the country to have a positive **balance of trade**. The Lekki Free Trade Zone (see **page 87**) has already attracted manufacturers of hair accessories, steel pipes, furniture and trucks. The jobs and taxes provided by these industries are helping the country to develop.

The changing political and trading relationships with the wider world

Kingdoms, in what is now known as Nigeria, were active in trade well before European traders arrived, but in the 18th century Portuguese and British ships arrived to trade. Close political and trade links with the UK developed when Nigeria was part of the British Empire, but now Nigeria mainly trades with Brazil, China, India, Japan, the US and the EU, and is a regional political leader in West Africa.

Environmental impacts of economic development

As Nigeria has developed, it has designated seven National Parks which aim to preserve, protect and manage vegetation and wild animals. As part of the United Nations, Nigeria is working towards the **Sustainable Development Goals**.

Hydro-power dams such as Asejire Dam have destroyed habitats as reservoirs filled and reduced river flow downstream. Deforestation has seen the loss of over 50% of Nigeria's forests due to farming, logging and the development of land.

See **page 114** for how development of the oil industry has led to habitat destruction in the Niger Delta.

Effects of economic development on the quality of life for the population

The impact of development on quality of life varies from place to place and between different ethnic groups. The north of the country is significantly less developed than the south and many urban areas face challenges, such as in Lagos (see **page 86**).

Nigeria's **Human Development Index (HDI)** improved from 0.467 in 2005 to 0.539 in 2019, reflecting improvements in wealth, health and education. However, this saw Nigeria ranked 161st out of 189 countries. Life expectancy was 45.67 years in 1982 but had risen to 55.44 years by 2022.

Types and impacts of international aid

Bilateral aid

The UK's planned budget for **bilateral aid** to Nigeria in 2019/20 was £220 million, with priorities including:

- Development of the north east of the country
- A health programme for mothers and babies
- A sanitation programme including hygiene and water

The Department for International Development in the UK stated that Nigeria is an important trading partner. Sometimes, bilateral aid deals can be linked to trading relationships.

Multilateral aid

Nigeria also receives **multilateral aid**, with **The World Bank** committing to spending $12.2 billion on the Country Partnership Strategy in 2021–2024. In the past, some **top-down** aid schemes supported by organisations like the World Bank have been criticised for not meeting the needs of the communities and people they are supposed to serve.

! Note

Bilateral aid comes directly from another government. **Multilateral** aid comes through international organisations. See **page 110**.

Charitable aid

Non-governmental organisations (NGOs) providing aid in Nigeria include international NGOs such as Oxfam but also those run by Nigerians such as the Tony Elumelu Foundation which supports youths and women in starting businesses. NGOs may promote **bottom-up** aid schemes, placing local communities at the heart of decision making.

Use a case study of a LIC or NEE to suggest how the manufacturing industry can stimulate economic development.   [6]

Nigeria is a NEE in West Africa which once depended upon the primary sector, trading in cash crops and oil, with little investment in the secondary sector. Political stability and the inclusion of Nigeria as a MINT country since 2011 have seen growing investment in manufacturing industries, an example being the development of the Lekki Free Trade Zone in Lagos State through Chinese investment. As manufacturers of steel pipes, furniture, trucks and more have set up on this zone, they have not only provided jobs and taxes, but have also stimulated a multiplier effect, buying products from other companies and also stimulating retail. This combines to have had a significant impact on economic development. Level 3 - Detailed: 6 marks. Refer to levels-based mark bands provided on page 178.

ECONOMIC FUTURES IN THE UK

The UK has seen major changes in its economy, with consequences for employment patterns and regional growth.

Causes of economic change

Before the industrial revolution, most people in the UK worked in farming, mining, fishing or forestry, but, following the industrial revolution from the 1750s, many people moved to the city to work in factories (**urbanisation**). From the 1970s, great change was happening again, this time due to:

Globalisation

Products such as coal and steel were being imported from overseas and sold at lower prices, undercutting UK producers.

Government policies

The Government decided to rationalise traditional industries, closing inefficient mines and factories and investing in a few more efficient sites

Deindustrialisation

Many **traditional industries** such as coal mines and steel works closed, leading to loss of jobs. Miners protested against government policy by striking and marching.

A disused mine

Moving towards a post-industrial economy

Service industries and the development of information technology

Whilst **traditional industries** were declining, new industries in the **tertiary** (service industries and finance) and **quaternary** (**information technology** and research) sectors were growing. Whereas traditional industries were located near to raw materials and near workers in the inner city, new industries located on the edge of cities to benefit from cheaper land, large spaces and good links to motorways and airports.

Stoke on Trent is famous for its potteries. Now many are tourist attractions and the shopping centre is called 'The Potteries'

Examples of developments in the post-industrial economy

Information technology: High tech businesses involved in software and web development may locate in science parks, but they are also often found in city centres as part of regeneration schemes. An example of this is The Engine Shed in Bristol's Temple Quarter (see **page 99**).

Service industries: Ranging from retail to fitness and beyond, service industries provide products and services to consumers. Now, retail often takes place online or in shopping malls such as Westfield, London, with malls aiming to provide a full leisure experience for visitors.

Finance: Bristol is a city known for its finance industries, including insurance companies, accountancy and banking. It is one of the main finance hubs in the UK, with 33 500 people employed in financial services in the city.

Research: Public and private sector organisations carry out research to develop new products. For example, pharmaceutical companies are always looking for new ways to use and develop their products. Research organisations are often found in science parks (see below).

Business and science parks

Business parks

Business parks developed in towns and cities, often near motorway junctions, providing sites including units and car parks, ready for businesses to move into. These parks include a mixture of uses, including manufacturing, warehouses, leisure organisations and offices. They often have hotels, restaurants and gyms to cater for the workers and visitors to the business parks.

Science parks

Science parks are more specialised than business parks, but share the characteristics of being on the edge of cities on sites with good access to transport. They are linked to universities and specialise in information technology and research. The first science park in the UK was developed in Cambridge in 1970 by Trinity College and there are now 130 companies there, including Astra Zeneca, Huawei and Toshiba. It is important to make the sites of science parks welcoming and good places to work as they are trying to attract highly qualified workers. See **page 120**.

CAMBRIDGE SCIENCE PARK

An example of an environmentally sustainable modern industrial development

CAMBRIDGE SCIENCE PARK
CELEBRATING 40 YEARS
OF COLLABORATION 1970 - 2010

Cambridge Science Parks sits on the north fringe of Cambridge. It has become Europe's most successful science park. A hotspot of technology companies, the park aspires to be as smart as those who work there.

Impacts of industry on the physical environment

Traditional industries had a major impact on the environment, with mines and quarries often causing air, water, land and noise pollution. Manufacturing also damaged the environment as fossil fuels were burnt to power machines, increasing greenhouse gas emissions and acid rain. Modern industries have choices to make; they may operate unsustainably, creating waste and contributing to emissions, or they may make sustainable choices to protect and enhance the environment now and in the longer term.

Cambridge Science Park has taken action to be more **environmentally sustainable**, including:

- Smart paving slabs. Nanotechnology breaks down nitrogen dioxide into harmless nitrates.

- Green spaces including lakes and woods.

- A renewable energy technologies centre was established on the Park in 2019.

- Old buildings which didn't meet sustainability standards are being replaced with low energy, low carbon buildings.

SOCIAL AND ECONOMIC CHANGES IN THE RURAL LANDSCAPE

Cities aren't the only places to have been affected by changes in the UK economy. **Rural** areas have seen changes due to **economic migration**. People may be **pushed** from some rural areas as they are remote and lack services, but others are **pulled** to rural areas if they are near enough to cities for people to **commute** to work.

Depopulation in Powys, mid Wales

- In 2019, Powys County Council found that an average of 1000 young people were leaving Powys each year (total population of Powys was 132 400 in 2018).

- Declining numbers of younger people have led to school closures and a reduction of health services in the county. Budgets are set using population forecasts and changes, so Powys is facing cuts.

- To tackle this, politicians have worked with young people to come up with priorities to reduce depopulation.

- These priorities include a focus on high quality education, new high paid, high skilled and green jobs, affordable homes, improved broadband and mobile phone signals, and free bus transport for the under 25s.

Population growth in South Cambridgeshire

- South Cambridgeshire is experiencing rapid growth, with a population of 156 000 in 2018 increasing by 8.8% to 169 800 in 2019 and predictions of a population of over 200 000 by 2036.

- Demand for housing has pushed house prices up to an average of £460 000 (England average is £228 000) and new housing estates are being developed to meet demand, often on **greenfield** sites.

- Higher prices make it difficult for local people to afford homes and some feel the character of their villages is changing as they become **suburbanised**.

IMPROVEMENTS AND DEVELOPMENTS IN ROAD AND RAIL INFRASTRUCTURE, PORT AND AIRPORT CAPACITY

Road infrastructure

Highways England announced a £27.4 billion investment in the road network in 2020, with £11 billion spending on repairing roads and £14 billion for improving the quality, capacity and safety of motorways and major A roads. Flagship projects included a new road and tunnel under the Thames to link Essex and Kent.

Airport capacity

The need to increase airport capacity in the UK is being challenged due to environmental concerns and a reduced need for business travel due to use of online meetings. A plan to build a third runway to increase the capacity of Heathrow Airport was approved by the government in 2018, but in 2021 key figures such as Lord Deben (chair of the Climate Change Committee) said "there is not any space for airport expansion".

Rail infrastructure

The Integrated Rail Plan (IRP) launched in 2021 includes a £96 billion package of upgrades and new construction in the Midlands and north of England, and three new high-speed lines (Northern Powerhouse Rail, HS2 East and HS2 West).

Port capacity

£400 million has been invested in the construction of Liverpool2 to improve the capacity of the Port of Liverpool. New technology is being used to make the port more efficient and able to cope with even the largest container ships.

THE NORTH-SOUTH DIVIDE

The areas which suffered from **deindustrialisation** in the UK were mainly in the north of England, whereas many of the new **high technology and research** developments have been in the South East.

Disparities

The South East has a third of the UK population but 45% of its economy and 42% of its wealth. Some say that this has led to a **north-south divide**. The State of the North 2021 study found that from 2014 to 2019 London had received £12 147 per person in funding whilst the figure in the North was £8 125.

Strategies used in an attempt to resolve regional differences

In 2022, the Department for Levelling Up, Housing and Communities said that they were providing a £4.8 billion Levelling Up Fund to close the gap between the regions. Local authorities (councils) were invited to bid for money for projects to tackle **urban deprivation**. One example is the Wirral, which received £20 million to transform the waterfront at Woodside and £80 million for regeneration and growth.

THE PLACE OF THE UK IN THE WIDER WORLD

Links

The UK is linked to the wider world through:

Electronic communication: Most people are connected to others across the world through email, social media and virtual meetings. However, there is a digital divide, and some are not as connected as others.

Trade: The exchange of goods between countries.

Culture: The UK is a multicultural country. It influences cultures across the world, and is influenced by them.

Transport: Airports such as Heathrow and ports such as Felixstowe and Liverpool2 connect the UK to the world, and the Channel Tunnel to mainland Europe.

Economic and political links

Links between the UK and the rest of the world have changed over time.

Britain ruled 24% of the land area of the world by 1920. The British Empire declined as countries became independent, but many ex-colonies stay connected to the UK through the **Commonwealth**.

The UK joined the European Economic Union (**a trade bloc**) in 1973. This became the **European Union (EU)** in 1993, with more political and social unity.

The UK left the EU in 2020. This ended rights of freedom of movement between the EU and the UK. The UK was free to make new deals with countries around the world.

1920   1993   2020

Assess the importance of economic and political links with the world to the UK economy. [9]

The UK was once linked to a vast Empire as an Imperial power. By the 1920s, the British Empire controlled 24% of the land area of the world. The British encouraged countries such as Nigeria to grow cash crops which were then brought to the UK to feed the growing population. Cotton from colonies was brought into ports such as Bristol, stimulating the growth of cotton mills through the multiplier effect, benefitting the UK economy. Although the British Empire declined in the 20th century, many countries that were colonies are still linked to the UK through the Commonwealth and are still linked through trade. In 1973, the UK joined the European Union (EU), becoming part of a trade bloc and so benefitting from free trade with other EU countries, which boosted the UK economy. Freedom of movement to work and live across the EU began in 1992, helping UK businesses find workers, especially in sectors such as farming and care. The UK left the EU in 2020; some think leaving the trade bloc will harm the economy, but others think the economy will be boosted by the government creating individual deals with different countries. Therefore, both economic and political links are extremely important to the UK economy. Mark bands on page 178.

EXAMINATION PRACTICE

1. Look at the world map on **page 106** showing the Human Development Index.
   Describe the distribution of countries with the highest HDI (0.800-1.000). [2]

2. Why is the Human Development Index seen as a better measure of development than
   Gross Domestic Product? [3]

3. Outline how **one** physical factor can lead to uneven development between countries. [2]

4. Explain how debt relief can reduce the development gap. [4]

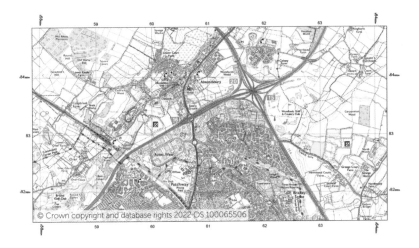

© Crown copyright and database rights 2022 OS 100065506

5. (a) Using the figure above, give the six figure grid reference for the centre of the
       motorway junction. [1]
    A. ☐ 585 835
    B. ☐ 618 838
    C. ☐ 607 824
    D. ☐ 638 833

   (b) Using the figure above, what is the main land use in grid square 58 84? [1]
    A. ☐ Housing
    B. ☐ Golf course
    C. ☐ Forest
    D. ☐ Playing fields

   Aztec West is a business park shown in grid squares 59 82 and 60 82.
   (c) Using the figure above, what is the direction from Aztec West to the motorway junction? [1]
    A. ☐ North west
    B. ☐ South west
    C. ☐ South
    D. ☐ North east

The following information is about the Aztec West business park.

> *Aztec West is a business park in the north of Bristol, close to the M4 and M5 motorways and the Almondsbury interchange motorway junction.*
>
> *The park was first set up in the 1980s with high tech buildings and landscaped grounds.*
>
> *There are now over 100 companies in Aztec West and over 7 000 people work there.*
>
> *The park includes a four star hotel, office villages and a central retail area as well as a wide range of businesses.*
>
> *Companies based in Aztec West include Nokia, Aardman, The Co-operative Legal Services, HSBC and Highways England.*

6. Suggest **two** benefits for businesses of moving to Aztec West.   [4]

7. Using an example, explain how modern industrial development can be more environmentally sustainable.   [6]

8. Assess the impact of economic changes on the rural landscape in the UK.   [9]

RESOURCE MANAGEMENT

Resources are a stock or supply of something that has a value or purpose. Key resources often include food, water and energy which are needed to survive. Resources are needed for a country to develop and to provide economic and social wellbeing to the population.

Most resources are not distributed equally around the globe. HICs often having greater access to resources in comparison to LICs, as HICs can afford to import them if they don't already have them.

Food

In many countries around the world **food** is in plentiful supply, however, in other countries food is a scarce resource. Nearly 1 billion people globally are **malnourished** as they don't have a high enough calorie intake on a regular basis. LICs may face food insecurity, with higher rates of malnutrition.

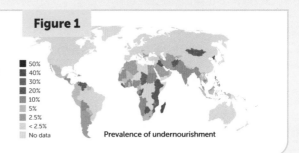

Figure 1

- 50%
- 40%
- 30%
- 20%
- 10%
- 5%
- 2.5%
- < 2.5%
- No data

Prevalence of undernourishment

Water

Water is a vital resource not only for consumption, but also for industrial and agricultural purposes. As the world's population increases, issues with water scarcity are growing. Some countries face economic **water scarcity**, which means they can't afford to extract from water sources or keep water clean, whilst others face physical water scarcity which is a lack of water available to use.

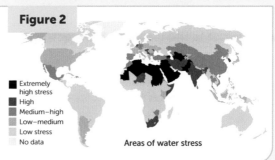

Figure 2

- Extremely high stress
- High
- Medium–high
- Low–medium
- Low stress
- No data

Areas of water stress

Energy

Energy is needed for many technologies and for the industrial development of an area. Historically, most countries used their own natural resources to produce energy, however energy is now traded worldwide.

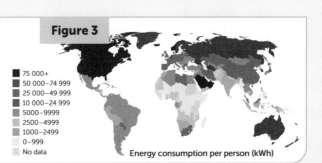

Figure 3

- 75 000+
- 50 000–74 999
- 25 000–49 999
- 10 000–24 999
- 5000–9999
- 2500–4999
- 1000–2499
- 0–999
- No data

Energy consumption per person (kWh)

Using **Figure 3**, suggest how energy consumption is linked to levels of development. [3]

The figure shows that energy consumption is often higher in places with higher levels of economic development, such as the USA and Canada.[1] Whereas consumption is lower in less economically developed countries, such as Kenya.[1] This suggests that the higher the development, the more energy is consumed.[1] This could be due to greater access to electronic goods which require energy to use them.[1]

FOOD IN THE UK

The population of the UK is growing and is expected to hit 70 million people by 2030. This means **demand** for food is increasing and, despite the UK having a strong agricultural sector, it is not enough to meet national demand. As a result, the UK **imports** around 45% of its food supply.

Wages

Food produced in the UK is often more expensive than imported food because workers are paid more and animal feed is expensive. Workers overseas may be paid much less.

Seasonal produce

People want access to seasonal produce, such as strawberries, in the UK all year round.

Why does the UK import food?

Yields

Yields (amounts grown) of UK crops can be poor due to the climate. Little can be grown outside in the cold winters and weather can be unpredictable, with storms and droughts affecting crops.

Demand

Demand has increased for exotic foods that can't be grown in the UK, such as bananas and cocoa beans.

What is the impact of importing food?

The distance food travels to get from the area it is grown, manufactured and sold, and then to where it is consumed is measured in **food miles**. Transporting food a long way is not only expensive, it also increases the **carbon footprint** (see page 152).

If farmers aren't paid enough or work in unfair conditions, they are being exploited. In some cases, farmers could be getting as little as 5% of the price we pay in the shop, with most profit going to the supermarket.

How is the UK responding to this challenge?

Agribusiness

Agribusiness is intensive farming with the purpose of maximising output of food and also profit. Lynford House Farm is a large arable (crops only) farm in East Anglia which farms wheat and potatoes. They use pesticides, fertilisers and highly efficient machinery to keep yields up, and labour costs down.

Organic produce

Organic produce is food grown without the use of artificial chemicals. Sales of organic food was worth £279 billion in 2021 following a 12.6% increase in 2020. Riverford Organic Farmers has capitalised on this growth, delivering around 45 000 organic produce boxes per week in 2018. The benefits of this are reduced food miles, support for local farmers and a strong link between grower and consumer.

Outline **one** advantage of buying locally grown food. [2]

Money goes straight to the farmer[1] to increase the profitability of the farm.[1] Decreases the food miles in the supply chain,[1] and therefore reduces CO_2 emissions.[1] People know where the food comes from,[1] which builds a connection between producers and consumers.[1]

WATER IN THE UK

What are the UK's water demands?

Demand for water has risen in the UK over time as the population has grown. People shower and wash clothes more often and industries and farms also use more water.

This is increasing the **water stress** in parts of England. Water stress is caused when the demand for water is higher than the supply. The south and east of England is hardest hit by water stress

Water can easily be saved through simple methods including using efficient technology in domestic appliances, increasing usage of recycled water and grey water, and using domestic water meters.

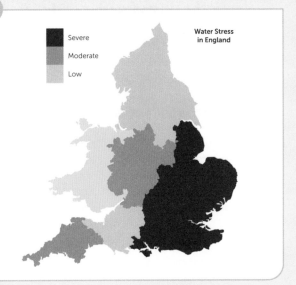

Water Stress in England

- Severe
- Moderate
- Low

Water quality and pollution management

Quality of water is just as important as the accessibility of water. The UK has a strict set of rules governing water quality. The Environment Agency is responsible for monitoring water quality in England, including rivers, lakes, the sea and groundwater, which can be polluted by agricultural chemicals and wastewater from industries. They issue licences for water abstraction and also environmental permits for waste management sites. If organisations cause pollution they can be prosecuted.

Strategies to improve water quality include:

- Regulating the amount and type of pesticides and fertilisers that can be used.
- Improving drainage systems to slow the movement of rainwater so that pollution can be broken down in the soil.

Water transfer

Water transfer schemes are designed to reduce the water stress in an area by moving water from areas of **water surplus** to areas of **water deficit**. This is done through a series of dams, reservoirs and canals. The UK Government proposed a series of water transfer projects to move water from the north of England to the south, especially London, but these plans were halted due to the economic and environmental costs of the project.

Explain **one** disadvantage of a water transfer scheme in the UK. [2]

Economic.[1] A water transfer project would have extremely high costs as a lot of the infrastructure would need to be built from scratch.[1]
Or: Environmental.[1] Habitats in the areas of the water transfer project could be disrupted due to changes, these habitats would need to be relocated or protected.[1]

ENERGY IN THE UK

How is the UK energy demand changing?

Consumption of energy in the UK is decreasing because of deindustrialisation and changes in technology, with a lot of new appliances being more energy efficient.

What is the UK's energy mix and how has it changed?

The UK used to be more self-sufficient in energy as it was using oil and gas reserves from the North Sea, but nearly 75% of known reserves have now been used. The **energy security** of the UK has decreased as its reliance on importing energy has grown.

As a result, the **energy mix** of the UK has changed. There has been a significant rise in the number of renewable energy sources contributing to the UK energy supply. However, oil and gas will still provide energy in the UK for the next few decades, so they will still form part of the mix.

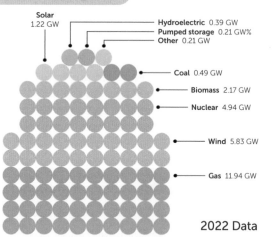

Solar 1.22 GW
Hydroelectric 0.39 GW
Pumped storage 0.21 GW%
Other 0.21 GW
Coal 0.49 GW
Biomass 2.17 GW
Nuclear 4.94 GW
Wind 5.83 GW
Gas 11.94 GW

2022 Data

Impacts of energy exploitation

Fracking

(Not used in UK as of 2022.)

What is it? Fracking uses high pressure liquids (water, sand and chemicals) to fracture shale rock and extract the gas.

➕ **Economic:** Brings jobs to areas where shale gas can be extracted.

➖ **Economic:** Very high cost to develop extraction sites.

➕ **Environmental:** Burning shale gas emits less carbon dioxide than coal.

➖ **Environmental:** Can pollute groundwater and cause small earthquakes.

Nuclear

What is it? Using the heat from nuclear fission to drive steam turbines, to produce electricity.

➕ **Economic:** Jobs to build and then to run the power station.

➖ **Economic:** Extremely high costs to develop and also to decommission (shut down).

➕ **Environmental:** Generating nuclear energy doesn't release greenhouse gasses.

➖ **Environmental:** Radioactive leaks can cause long term damage and waste has to be carefully disposed of.

Wind power

What is it? Harnessing the power of the wind to produce electricity.

➕ **Economic:** One of the lowest cost energy sources.

➖ **Economic:** Some locations aren't cost effective.

➕ **Environmental:** Renewable and non-polluting.

➖ **Environmental:** Some find wind turbines ugly and don't like the noise. Bird strike.

GLOBAL DEMAND FOR FOOD

Global patterns of calorie intake

Globally, calorie intake is higher in HICs, such as the USA, Canada and the majority of Europe, whereas places in Sub-Saharan Africa are consuming fewer calories than recommended. This leads to **undernourishment**.

Food consumption has increased due to a rapidly rising **global population** and **economic development**. Improved technology allows greater access to food and more people can afford to consume larger quantities of food.

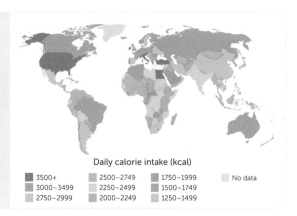

Daily calorie intake (kcal)

3500+	2500–2749	1750–1999	No data
3000–3499	2250–2499	1500–1749
2750–2999	2000–2249	1250–1499

Global patterns of food supply

Areas which have poor supplies of food are likely to face issues such as **malnourishment** (not getting the right balance of nutrition) as well as undernourishment.

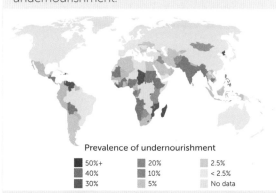

Prevalence of undernourishment

50%+	20%	2.5%
40%	10%	< 2.5%
30%	5%	No data

The Hunger Map was designed by the World Food Programme to highlight areas facing this problem, including Sub-Saharan Africa, Central America and parts of Asia.

Suggest **one** reason why countries in Sub-Saharan Africa face more food insecurity than European countries. [2]

Climate.[1] A drier climate in Sub-Saharan Africa will mean that growing crops is less reliable due to water shortages.[1]

Or: Poverty.[1] Sub-Saharan countries are less economically developed so they may not be able to afford to import as many food goods.[1]

Food security

When a country is **food secure** people can afford to buy or produce enough food to lead a healthy life.

If a country produces more food than it needs, then it has a **food surplus** and it can export excess to other countries.

If a country has less food than it needs, then it has a **food deficit** and will need to import food to make up the difference. If a country is very dependent on importing food, then it is **food insecure**. If a country in deficit can't afford to import food, its population will suffer.

FACTORS THAT IMPACT FOOD SUPPLY

Climate

Areas with different climates will be suited to different farming techniques and will result in different yields. Areas along the tropics, for example, are dry, reducing opportunities for farming.

Water stress

When water scarcity limits supplies, there may be conflict over who uses the water and for what. In the Sahel in Africa, desertification means some farmers are being forced off the land into cities.

Poverty

The poorest communities are often those with the lowest food security. They may not be able to afford to buy food and may also struggle to grow it if they can't afford fertiliser.

Technology

HICs and NEEs may use technology to increase food production through the use of machinery, genetic modification of crops or irrigation systems. In LICs, use of high technology approaches may be limited due to availability, unreliable energy supply and cost, but **intermediate technology** is making a big difference in many locations.

Pests and diseases

Areas with different climates are also prone to different pests and diseases. In wet locations plants may suffer from rot, whilst in the tropics diseases such as sleeping sickness seriously affect livestock.

Conflict

Wars and political instability can mean that large areas of agricultural land are abandoned as people flee. Imported food may be limited if sanctions are placed on a country to try to persuade the government to change its policies.

Explain the impact of climate change on global food supplies.   [4]

Climate change is threatening food supplies globally. It is causing more extremes in the global climate, meaning that areas which are already arid are likely to face a more extreme climate and this can cause these areas to face further water stress and potential desertification. This water stress may mean that these areas do not have the resources required for agricultural development. Climate change can also cause pests and diseases to spread around the world, currently these are mostly common in the tropics, but with a warming world it is likely that these can spread further north and south of the Equator. Mark of 4 given in accordance with the mark bands on page 178.

IMPACTS OF FOOD INSECURITY

Famine

Famine is an extreme lack of food leading to malnutrition, starvation and often death.

Yemen famine   2016-present

Causes

The Yemeni civil war led to a decline in food production.

The Saudi blockade destroyed fishing boats and agricultural land meaning that food production declined.

Consequences

More than 85,000 deaths of children since it started in 2016.

Cholera outbreak in Yemen.

Soil erosion

Soil erosion is the removal of the more fertile top layers of soil due to wind or the movement of water. It is linked to food insecurity through:

Overgrazing

Reduces the amount of vegetation, making the soil more vulnerable to erosion.

Over-cultivation of land

Nutrients are used but not replaced, exhausting the soil.

Deforestation

Removes the protective covering of the trees and causes an increase in the surface run off of water as interception is reduced.

Undernutrition

Undernourishment means not consuming enough nutrients to be healthy. If people don't have enough food to provide the energy for school or work, it can weaken their immune system. Different medical conditions are associated with a lack of different nutrients. For example, anaemia is caused by a lack of iron and kwashiorkor is caused by a lack of protein. Undernourished children can't develop properly.

Rising prices

Rising food prices are related to increased costs of farming, such as the use of chemicals and fertiliser, processing and transportation. This can mean the poorest in society can no longer afford staple foods such as rice, corn and wheat.

Social unrest

Increased food prices can lead to social unrest, sometimes known as food riots. In 2016, in Venezuela there were food riots throughout the capital city of Caracas due to a steep fall in oil prices causing massive inflation in food prices throughout the country. Over 400 people were arrested.

State **one** social consequence of a country having a limited food supply.   [1]

One from: Social unrest,[1] famine,[1] undernutrition.[1]

STRATEGIES TO INCREASE FOOD SUPPLY

Irrigation

Irrigation strategies involve the construction of artificial dams, reservoirs and canals to increase the supply of water in areas suitable for agricultural industries.

These can be expensive **infrastructure** projects but can also be done on a smaller scale. Overuse of a water resource can lead to conflict between users, and when water evaporates salt can be left behind on fields.

Biotechnology

Genetic modification can change crops or livestock to make them more productive or to be resistant to conditions such as droughts.

Appropriate tech

Technology should be suitable for an area, using skills and materials that are easily acquired and cheap. Communities are involved to make sure any technology meets their needs and is accessible.

Suggest **one** benefit of using appropriate technology to increase food supply in a LIC. [2]

Appropriate technology can easily be maintained by people in LICs[1] so will continue to work in the long term, making it sustainable.[1]

Aeroponics and hydroponics

Both these techniques can be used to grow produce all year around, but electricity costs may be high to run the pumps required.

Aeroponics

Uses a nutrient rich mist to grow plants indoors. This uses less water than traditional agricultural techniques and allows small scale farmers to increase yields.

Hydroponics

Uses water full of nutrients to feed plants growing in gravel.

Plants grown with aeroponics

The new green revolution

The first green revolution involved use of genetically modified crops to increase yields in India. Now there is more of a focus on sustainability, including:

- Soil conservation
- Water harvesting and irrigation systems
- Use of science to improve the quality of seeds and livestock
- Use of efficient technology

INDUS BASIN IRRIGATION SCHEME (IBIS)

An example of a large scale agricultural development

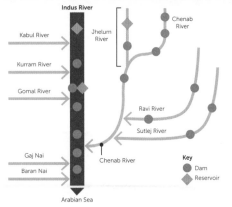

Advantages

➕ 40% more land can be farmed which has improved food security.

➕ Increased crop yields e.g. ↑36% for wheat.

➕ HEP generated by the main dams has increased energy availability and therefore improved energy security.

➕ New food products are available for local populations, leading to a more varied diet.

Features

In Pakistan, the **IBIS** is the largest continuous irrigation scheme in the world with:

- 3 large dams and 100+ smaller dams.
- 12 link canals to transfer water between rivers.
- Smaller canals to distribute water to the drier agricultural land in the south of Pakistan.
- 1.6 million km of ditches and streams providing water for farming.

Disadvantages

➖ Conflicts over how much water is used by different farmers.

➖ Evaporation leads to a large amount of water being lost.

➖ As water evaporates from fields it leaves salt behind.

➖ The upkeep of the reservoirs and dams is expensive.

'A large scale agricultural development can bring both advantages and disadvantages.'
Explain this statement using an example you have studied. [6]

The Indus Basin Irrigation System is located in Pakistan in South Asia. It starts in the Tibetan Plateau and flows south through Pakistan. It is a large scale irrigation system aimed at improving the food supply in this area. The system has many advantages. It has improved the food security in Pakistan as more land is now available for cultivation. This has also meant that the dietary variety has increased as new fruits, vegetables and proteins, such as fish have been made available. However, the system has disadvantages. Farmers frequently use an unfair amount of water, causing farmers further downstream to be limited in their water supply. This is not helped by poor irrigation techniques being used which can cause a large amount of water to be lost through evaporation.

A SUSTAINABLE FOOD RESOURCE FUTURE

Organic farming

Organic farming involves growing crops or rearing livestock without the use of artificial chemicals and fertilisers. People often pay a premium (more money) for organic produce.

Urban farming initiatives

Farming in a built up area can take many forms:

- Allotments where people grow their own food.
- Community gardens or farms where people share the work and the produce.
- Warehouses converted to use aeroponics to grow vegetables in city centres.

Having healthy food available in cities can improve diets whilst also enhancing the environment.

Permaculture

Permaculture is a way of farming that uses natural features and patterns of an ecosystem to produce food, including:

- Harvesting rainwater to use in the watering of crops.
- Rotation of crops to allow nutrients to re-enter the soil and maintain fertility.
- Managing woodland to provide habitats for smaller organisms.
- Keeping animals such as sheep, pigs and bees without using intensive techniques.

Fish and meat from sustainable sources

Fish

Overfishing is caused by demand from a growing population but also by technology such as drag nets and intensive fishing. An alternative approach is using quotas (limits on the numbers of fish caught) so that the fish species can repopulate without being wiped out.

Meat

Meat from sustainable sources will often be produced in small scale farms using techniques such as free-range livestock farming or organic methods. Productivity is lower, leading to higher prices, but the meat is often of a higher quality.

Reduced waste and losses

Nearly one third of all the food produced around the world ends up being wasted. This can happen at all stages in the production and selling of food. Most of this waste tends to be in HICs where there is a food surplus.

Ways to reduce the amount of food wasted:

- Have clearly labelled 'use by' dates on packaging. (Not 'best before dates'.)
- Improve storage of food in farms, transport depots and shops so damage is limited.
- Seal food in containers once opened so the freshness can be maintained for a longer period of time.

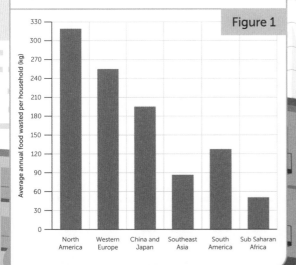

Figure 1

Seasonal food consumption

Before improvements in transport made mass imports of food possible, people in the UK could only buy fruit and vegetables when they were in season. For example, strawberries can be harvested in the UK from June to September, but people can now buy them at Christmas because they are imported from places such as Spain.

Buying food in season means that it can be produced in the UK, supporting local farmers and reducing food miles.

1. Figure 1 shows annual food waste by region. Use this figure to describe global trends in food waste. [2]

2. State the difference between the amount of food wasted in Western Europe and South America. Show your working. [1]

   1. *Figure 1 shows that the HIC and NEE regions typically have a much higher rate of food waste than LIC regions.[1] For example, over 300 kg/household of food is wasted in North America, whereas less than 50 kg/household is wasted in Sub Saharan Africa.[1]*

   2. *Europe has a figure of 255. (±3) Latin South America has a figure of 128. (±2) This means a difference of 127. (±4)[1]*

SAND DAMS IN KENYA

An example of a local scheme in a LIC to increase sustainable supplies of food

What are sand dams?

Sand dams are barriers constructed across **ephemeral streams** with a sandy river bed. Sand builds up behind the dam. Water is trapped in the sand, protected from evaporation and kept clean. People can dig down into the sand to collect the water. A river which would normally provide water for two weeks can provide water for several months if it has a sand dam.

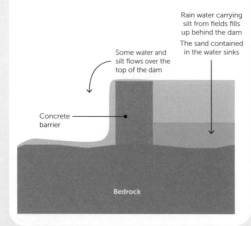

Some water and silt flows over the top of the dam

Rain water carrying silt from fields fills up behind the dam

The sand contained in the water sinks

Concrete barrier

Bedrock

Features

Excellent Development is a small NGO that works with communities to build sand dams, terrace the land and plant trees. This is an example of **appropriate technology**; it can easily be built and maintained by local people. For another example, see **page 111**.

Advantages

➕ Water lasts far longer in the area, meaning that the local population has a clean supply of water, and don't have to travel further to access this vital resource.

➕ Terracing the land has reduced soil erosion in the local area.

➕ Crop yields and food security are increased for local populations.

➕ Trees make the microclimate wetter which will raise the water table, enabling more vegetation to grow. Newly planted trees may also provide fruit which increases the food supply in an area.

Explain how food security can be increased sustainably in an LIC or NEE. Use an example of a local scheme to support your answer. [4]

Sand dams in Kenya are an example of a local sustainable scheme that has increased food supply in the area. Sand dams work by allowing water and sand to build up behind the barrier, the sand acts as a filter, but also prevents evaporation. This means that water that is usually lost either to runoff or evaporation is kept in the local area. This water can be used in agriculture to increase the yield of crops, and therefore increase food security in the local area. Trees can also be planted, these can provide fruits which also increases food security.

This levels-based question should be marked in accordance with the mark bands provided on page 178.

GLOBAL DEMAND FOR WATER

Demand for water resources is rising globally but supply can be insecure, which may lead to conflict.

Global patterns of water surplus and deficit

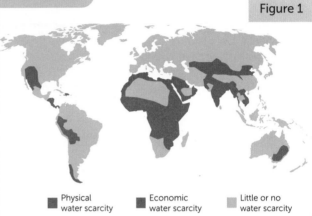

Figure 1

Having a water surplus means that, in an area, the supply of water is higher than the demand. Having a water deficit means that the supply of water is lower than the demand.

This can vary for physical reasons, such as the area having a drier climate, (meaning there are lower levels of rainfall) or it could be due to human reasons, such as having a high population density or having an increasing need for water for industrial or agricultural usage.

■ Physical water scarcity ■ Economic water scarcity ■ Little or no water scarcity

Water security

Water security

Water security means having access to a clean and affordable supply of water. This water can then be used to sustain wellbeing, good health and economic development.

Water insecurity

Water insecurity means not having good access to a clean and affordable supply of water. This means that the wellbeing of the area's population may not be met, and economic development may be limited.

- Countries that have below 1000m³ of water per person per year are defined as having **water scarcity**.
- Countries that have below 1700m³ of water per person per year are defined as having **water stress**.
- Countries that have below 2500m³ of water per person per year are defined as being **water vulnerable**.

Figure 1 shows global physical and economic water scarcity. Describe the distribution of areas of economic water scarcity in the figure. [2]

A large area experiencing economic water scarcity is found in Sub-Saharan Africa,[1] whilst there are also areas along the west of South America and in parts of Asia.[1]

WATER SUPPLY

Why is water consumption increasing?

Water consumption is increasing for several different reasons. The major reason has been due to a **rising global population**. The global population is expected to reach almost 9 billion people by 2035.

Water demand is also increasing because of **economic development**. As countries develop, the demand for vital resources increases as water is used in most industrial settings. Agriculture is very water intensive, and with global food demand due to rise by about 70%, the amount of water needed for irrigation systems and food processing will also increase. Energy production also uses water; global energy demand is expected to increase by 50% by 2035.

Factors affecting water availability

Geology

Whether a rock is impermeable or permeable changes the availability of water. In areas with permeable rocks there if often less surface water but aquifers (underground water) develop. 70% of London's water supply comes from a chalk aquifer in the sub-surface of the city. Impermeable rocks will often have more surface water, but less groundwater.

Limited infrastructure

Some places may have plenty of rainfall but not have the infrastructure to keep stored water clean or to transport it, leading to water insecurity.

Poverty

In many parts of the world poorer people have no access to mains water systems, often making water more expensive to access as it has to be bought from tankers or shops. People who can't afford this may be forced to use unsafe water, leading to disease.

Climate

Hot, dry areas (dominated by high pressure systems) will have less surface water available as there is little precipitation and high evaporation. People often rely on groundwater in aquifers in these areas. See **page 13** for the global atmospheric circulation system.

Over-abstraction

It is fine to use water from rivers, lakes and aquifers as long as it is being replaced by water from precipitation, but if this isn't the case, water sources can dry up as the water table drops and land may sink (subsidence).

Pollution of supply

Sewage waste and chemical run off from industry and agriculture has led to some water supplies becoming heavily polluted, making them unusable.

Outline **one** reason why some countries have limited availability of water. [2]

Poor infrastructure[1] because it limits their ability to extract water, store water and also to transport water to households.[1] Geology[1] because different types of rock will determine if water is stored in an aquifer or as surface water.[1] Two marks if one reason is stated and then developed.

IMPACTS OF WATER INSECURITY

Waterborne diseases and water pollution

Drinking water that has become contaminated by chemicals, fertilisers or sewage may lead to outbreaks of harmful waterborne diseases, such as cholera. A clean water source is difficult to find in some areas and people may have to travel a long way to access these sources. Collecting water is often left to women or children in a household, sometimes preventing children from going to school.

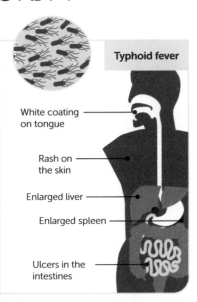

Typhoid fever

White coating on tongue

Rash on the skin

Enlarged liver

Enlarged spleen

Ulcers in the intestines

Water pollution in Nigeria

70% of Nigerians have access to basic water supplies, but pollutants contaminate more than half of these supplies. This increases disease from typhoid fever, diarrhoea, and dysentery. Diarrhoea is the second biggest killer of children <5 in Nigeria.

Food production

70% of the global water supply goes towards agriculture and food production, so water insecurity can also lead to food insecurity. Areas with poor water security may have to rely on importing food from other countries.

Industrial output

Some industries require a lot of water for cooling or production. A lack of water can make production much less effective, limiting economic development in an area. Water insecurity in NEEs is particularly harmful as these countries are dependent upon rapid industrialisation for the growth of their economies.

Potential for conflict where demand exceeds supply

Water sources, such as rivers, aquifers and groundwater, aren't limited to national and political borders. When a source is shared by several countries, tensions can be caused by:

Dams and reservoirs

These can cause a decrease in the flow of water down a river, but this can also have other environmental effects such as increased salinisation and decreasing water quality. For example, Turkey is developing a large scale infrastructure project by building large dams across the Tigris and Euphrates rivers. This has caused issues with water supply and quality downstream in countries such as Iraq and Syria. See **page 135.**

Pollution

Pollution in rivers caused by others upstream can lead to conflict and tension as it can have an impact on the health of people. For example, indigenous populations in the Malaysian Rainforest have seen a decrease in their quality of life as TNCs have polluted their water supply.

Explain **one** human impact of water insecurity   [2]

Health.[1] Water insecurity can impact the health of local populations causing an increase in health issues such as waterborne diseases.[1] War[1] can be caused due to fighting between countries over access to water supplies.[1]

STRATEGIES TO INCREASE WATER SUPPLY

Diverting water and increasing storage

Water can be diverted to replenish the supplies in storage, such as in aquifers or deep reservoirs. This is useful in an area which has infrequent rainfall, or where surface water quickly evaporates, but people in the source area may resent others using 'their' water.

Dams and reservoirs

Dams are used to control the flow of water in a river, with reservoirs behind them used for storing volumes of water. Water can be released during dry spells to keep rivers flowing and to ensure there is enough water for irrigation. Dams can also be used to produce hydroelectricity.

Large dams are extremely expensive to build and maintain. They can also cause the displacement of a large number of people in the reservoir area behind the dam. During the construction of the Three Gorges Dam in China nearly 1.3 million people were forced to move.

Desalination

Desalination is the process of removing salt from seawater, creating fresh water to drink. This process is expensive and energy intensive, so is only used where the water supply is extremely insecure and where there is enough affordable energy. Some of the largest desalination plants are found in Saudi Arabia, UAE and Israel, producing anywhere between 500 000 m³ and 1 000 000 m³ of freshwater per day. There are many disadvantages of desalination, such as increased carbon emissions, waste product and the need to transport freshwater inland.

Bhumibol Dam, Thailand

Water transfers

These infrastructure projects move water from areas of water surplus to areas of water deficit. See the China South-North Project on the next page.

---

1. State **one** social disadvantage of a strategy that can be used to increase water supply [1]
2. State **one** economic advantage of a strategy that can be used to increase water supply. [1]

1. *Displacement of people due to construction of dams and reservoirs.*[1]
2. *One from: Increased water supplies can be used to irrigate crops*[1] */ can be used in industrial development.*[1]

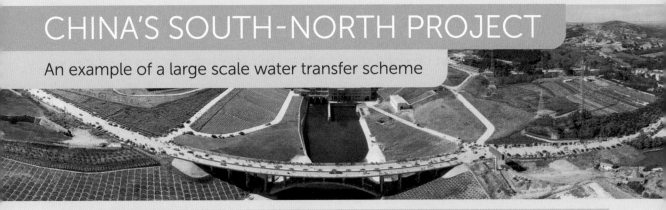

CHINA'S SOUTH-NORTH PROJECT

An example of a large scale water transfer scheme

Location

Situated between the Yangtze River Basin in the humid south of China and the Yellow River Basin in the more arid northern region.

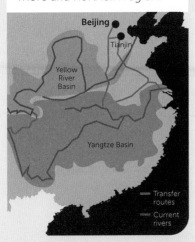

Why is it needed?

China has seen most of its industrial economic growth occur in the northern plains of China around the cities of Beijing and Tianjin. These cities have extremely high water demand but the supply is much lower. Beijing has exhausted a lot of its existing groundwater supplies so the transfer project is needed to maintain this growth as well as to support the population.

Features

The project, originally planned in 1952, focused on connecting the two main rivers of China through three main artificial canals: the western, central and eastern canals. The eastern route is 1,155km long and was completed in 2013. The central route is 1,267km long and opened in 2014 after delays. The western route is in the planning stages, and will controversially cross the Bayankala mountains through a series of canals and tunnels. It is expected to be completed in 2050, nearly 100 years after the project was first proposed.

Advantages

⊕ Increased availability of water in the major northern cities of China. This can supply industrial, agricultural and domestic uses.

⊕ Helping China cope with the pressure of climate change, water pollution and frequent periods of drought.

⊕ Reducing the rates of subsidence (land sinking) in Beijing due to over abstraction of water.

Disadvantages

⊖ Predicted cost of around $62 bn.

⊖ Over 300 000 people displaced by the construction of dams.

⊖ Risk of increasing pollution from industrial development along the eastern route, meaning that water is not fit for consumption.

⊖ Recent droughts in the humid south of China have shown that water is still insecure, and that there might not be enough water for local populations, let alone people living long distances away.

A SUSTAINABLE FUTURE FOR WATER

A range of strategies can be used to work together towards a more sustainable future for water.

Groundwater management

Supplies of water underground in **aquifers** can be managed effectively. Water needs to be abstracted in a way that is sustainable. As water is removed from the aquifer, time needs to be allowed for it to recharge.

Water conservation

Water conservation means using water more efficiently; this can be done individually or on a much larger scale by:

- Reducing leakages from pipes
- Improving education around the sustainable use of water.
- Using water meters to improve awareness of how much water is being used.
- Using water efficient technologies and upgrading older appliances such as washing machines and dishwashers to more water efficient models.

Water recycling

Recycling involves reusing wastewater after it has been chemically treated, in areas such as irrigation or within industrial processes.

This is common in a lot of energy production industries, such as nuclear energy, where recycled water is used for cooling. This means that more fresh water is available for domestic use, increasing the water security in an area.

Greywater

Greywater is taken from water sources in the home after use, such as that from washing machines, dishwashers, baths and showers. This water is stored in a tank on the property and is then reused for irrigation or use in gardens. This can have benefits for the garden as it may contain natural minerals and fertilisers for plant or crop growth. Water from toilets cannot be used as this is considered black water. See urban sustainability on **page 100**.

Suggest **one** reason why using water sustainably is important. [2]

Using water sustainably is important because it helps reduce the amount of freshwater being used[1] which can help increase water security in an area.[1]

WAKEL RIVER BASIN PROJECT

An example of a local sustainable water scheme in a NEE

Location

The Wakel River Basin is located in Rajasthan in NW India, in one of the poorest and driest areas of the country.

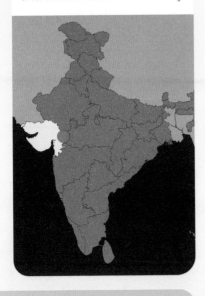

An ephemeral river is usually dry, but only flows seasonally or after rainfall or with snow meltwater.

Current Issues with water supply

The area gets less than 250mm of rainfall per year. The area is also very warm, so the little rainfall it does get is often lost through evaporation.

There is no regulation of the water in the area. This has meant that supplies are often over-abstracted, leading to groundwater levels falling and salinisation of water increasing. Some wells have also dried up.

Crops can't be reliably irrigated as the water supply is irregular, leading to food insecurity.

How are water supplies being increased?

There are three main methods being used:

Taankas: Large underground tanks which are filled when it rains. They store water and reduce evaporation.

Johed: Small earth dams that capture rainwater, allowing the water to be absorbed and helping to raise the water table. Previously ephemeral rivers sometimes start to flow year around.

Pats: Stone and mud bunds (dams) divert water into irrigation channels used by farmers to irrigate fields.

The United States Agency for International Development (USAID) has provided aid money for this project. It is a bottom-up project, meaning that the communities are heavily involved in the process. They are educated on how the system works and what they can do to increase water security in the area. See **page 110** for more on aid.

There are also Non-Governmental Organisations (NGOs), such as WaterHarvest, working with communities in Rajasthan on similar projects.

GLOBAL DEMAND FOR ENERGY

Global distribution of energy consumption

Energy security depends on two factors, the supply of energy and the consumption of energy. If a country has a higher supply than demand it has an **energy surplus**. If it has higher demand than supply it has an **energy deficit**. Countries with an energy deficit, or countries that depend highly on imported energy, are **energy insecure**.

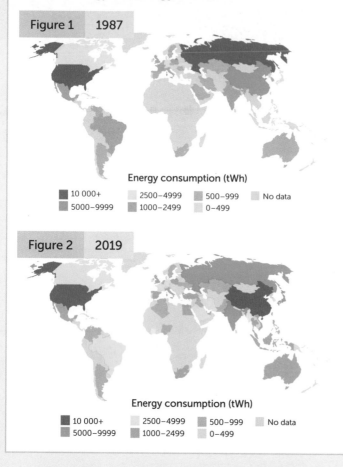

Figure 1   1987

Energy consumption (tWh)

■ 10 000+   ■ 2500–4999   ■ 500–999   □ No data
■ 5000–9999   ■ 1000–2499   ■ 0–499

Figure 2   2019

Energy consumption (tWh)

■ 10 000+   ■ 2500–4999   ■ 500–999   □ No data
■ 5000–9999   ■ 1000–2499   ■ 0–499

1. Figure 2 shows energy consumption in 2019. Describe the distribution of energy consumption shown in the figure.   [2]

2. Using Figures 1 and 2, give **one** difference between the energy consumption in 2019 and energy consumption in 1987.   [2]

> 1.   *Countries in Africa consume less energy than most other areas of the world.[1] The highest energy consumption is in countries with the largest populations, e.g. the USA and China.[1]*
>
>   Two marks for two separate elements of distribution.
>
>   No marks for explanations.
>
> 2.   *More countries in North Africa and the Middle East have increased energy consumption since 1987.[1]*

Why is energy consumption increasing?

Like other resources, the consumption of energy is increasing due to the **growing global population**, which is expected to reach roughly 9 billion people by 2035.

Economic development typically requires an increase in energy consumption, so as countries around the world develop, the demand for energy increases. This could be for domestic use, but often the rise is because of industrial use.

Energy supplies are more readily available as **new technologies** have allowed for the cheaper production of energy.

ENERGY SUPPLY

Factors affecting energy supply

Technology

Developments in technology means that areas that were previously inaccessible can now be used to produce oil and gas. Countries with poor access to technology may struggle to exploit resources and rely on other countries or TNCs for access to energy sources.

Economic factors

The costs of **exploitation and production** are high. Energy sources often require a high level of investment to be extracted, and the infrastructure associated is also very costly. This means that countries which don't have the capital (money) to invest may not be able to access these sources themselves and become reliant on investment from TNCs to access energy sources.

Example: Nuclear power stations are extremely expensive to build and require a lot of planning and investment. Hinkley Point C in south west England was first proposed as the site of a new nuclear reactor in 2010. Construction didn't start until 2018, and the project isn't expected to be completed until June 2026. It will cost around £20 billion and produce energy for 60 years.

Political factors

If a country is seen as politically unstable it may discourage other countries or TNCs from investing in the exploitation of energy sources.

Example: Venezuela has seen a dramatic decrease in its ability to export oil over recent years due to its political instability and sanctions from the USA.

Physical factors

The availability of fossil fuels is dependent on the geology of an area. If an area doesn't meet the correct conditions, then fossil fuels may not be available, or they may not be accessible.

Climate

Renewable energy sources, such as solar, wind and hydroelectric power (HEP), rely on the availability of sunshine, wind and water. It is important to consider which type of renewable power is suitable in each climate e.g. solar panels are suited to places on the tropics as they have intense sunlight and fewer clouds.

Distribution of gas

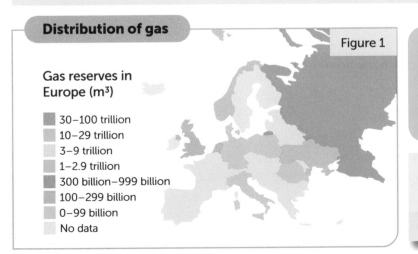

Figure 1

Gas reserves in Europe (m³)

- 30–100 trillion
- 10–29 trillion
- 3–9 trillion
- 1–2.9 trillion
- 300 billion–999 billion
- 100–299 billion
- 0–99 billion
- No data

Some countries that are in tectonically active zones may be able to use geothermal energy to produce energy. Nearly 65% of Iceland's energy is from geothermal sources.

Using Figure 1, state the range of gas reserves found in the United Kingdom. [1]

100-299 billion m³.[1]

IMPACTS OF ENERGY INSECURITY

Exploration of difficult and environmentally sensitive areas

There are many energy sources that have not been accessed due to areas being hostile or technology not being advanced enough to access them. Many of these hostile areas are also seen as environmentally sensitive areas with a unique environment that people see a need to preserve.

One area at the centre of debate has been the Arctic, which is believed to have many natural resources, such as oil and gas reserves. Some people are concerned that exploiting these resources could cause irreversible damage to the ecosystems and wildlife in the area, especially if something went wrong, such as an oil spill.

Economic and environmental costs

Finding and exploring new sources of fossil fuels or developing large scale energy systems, such as nuclear power stations, is extremely expensive. If costs are cut too far, the results can be devastating, such as oil spills. Choices made about energy production affect the cost of energy to the consumer.

Industrial output

Manufacturing industries have a high demand for energy; energy shortages can cause a decrease in productivity which can have severe economic impacts on an area. Energy insecurity often means lower industrial output.

Impacts on food production

Using food resources to create biofuels can force food prices up. Staple foods such as sugar cane and maize have seen their prices rise due to the creation of biofuels. Land is also being used for production of biofuels instead of agriculture, reducing food supplies in some places.

Potential for conflict where demand exceeds supply

Tensions can rise between countries over energy resources. The Gulf Wars and Iraq Wars can be seen as driven by western society's fears over oil shortages. Tensions are high in Eastern Africa over the damming of the Nile River in Ethiopia to generate hydroelectric power as countries downstream, such as Egypt, are concerned about their water supplies.

Explain **one** economic impact of energy insecurity. [2]

If industries can't access reliable energy, they will be less productive[1] which will affect the economy and could cause a loss of jobs.[1]

STRATEGIES TO INCREASE ENERGY SUPPLY

Having a mixture of energy sources prevents a country becoming too dependent on a single source. This is called the energy mix. A good energy mix uses a variety of different energy sources.

Non-renewable energy sources

Non-renewable resources have a finite supply. These include fossil fuels and nuclear energy.

Fossil fuels

Although these are finite (will run out) there are still supplies available. Prices increase when demand outstrips supply.

- Fossil fuels include coal, gas and oil.
- They are used as the primary source of energy in many countries.
- They produce CO_2 when burnt.
- They also release sulphur dioxide which causes acid rain.

Nuclear power

This uses radioactive materials to fuel nuclear fission. This heats water, to create steam which turns turbines to produce electricity.

- Radioactive fuels such as uranium and plutonium have a relatively low cost per unit of energy produced, as little is needed.
- There is a lot of opposition to nuclear power due to safety concerns and the cost of development.
- Radioactive waste can stay harmful for an extremely long time.

Explain **one** benefit of having a good energy mix. [2]

A benefit of a good energy mix is not being too reliant on a single source.[1] This means that if the supply from one source decreases, there are others to use as alternatives.[1]

Renewable energy sources

Biomass

Plant material is burnt to generate energy.

Wind

Wind is available everywhere, weather dependent, and costs of turbines have dropped significantly in recent years.

Hydro (HEP)

HEP uses dams and the flow of water to produce electricity.

Tidal

Tidal barrages cost a lot of money to develop, and they disturb habitats. They can produce massive amounts of electricity from the regular tidal flow.

Geothermal

Geothermal energy is limited to areas which are tectonically active, but provides cheap energy in these areas.

Wave

Continual movement of waves up and down can be used to generate electricity.

Solar

Solar power has great potential in LICs where lots of sunlight is available.

GAS

An example of fossil fuel extraction

Natural gas forms from the remains of plants and animals buried in ocean sediments over millions of years. Extreme heat and pressure break the organic compounds down into hydrocarbons, releasing methane in the process. Gas is then extracted from these reservoirs, typically found deep underground.

Global reserves of natural gas

Reserves of natural gas are found all over the world, with the majority of remaining reserves found in Russia, Iran and Qatar. Supplies are expected to last until at least 2060, or longer if new reserves are found.

Shale gas is the newest form of gas to be extracted. The largest reserves are believed to be in China, Argentina and Algeria.

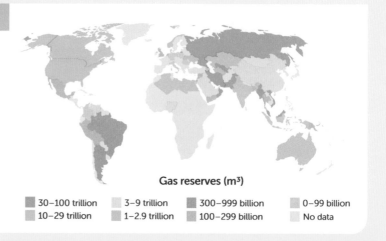

Gas reserves (m³)

30–100 trillion	3–9 trillion	300–999 billion	0–99 billion
10–29 trillion	1–2.9 trillion	100–299 billion	No data

Advantages of extracting natural gas

There are several advantages of using gas over other fossil fuels:

- Natural gas is the cleanest fossil fuel, producing less CO_2 than oil and coal.

- Natural gas is more easily transported and stored than other fossil fuels.

- Natural gas is often seen as safe energy.

Disadvantages of extracting natural gas

Large reserves of natural gas are located in countries that are politically unstable.

Despite being the cleanest form of fossil fuel, it still causes pollution through CO_2 and methane emissions.

Fracking is a highly controversial form of gas extraction due to environmental concerns, such as water contamination and earthquakes.

Extracting shale gas in the UK

Shale gas is extracted from shale rocks using a water, chemical and aggregates solution that is pumped under pressure into the rocks. This helps open cracks in the rock so the gas can be pumped out. This process is known as hydraulic fracturing, more commonly known as fracking.

In the UK, shale gas exploitation has been proposed for many years, however there is currently no commercial shale gas drilling due to a moratorium from the government. This is because of environmental concerns such as groundwater pollution, use of protected landscapes and small magnitude earthquakes.

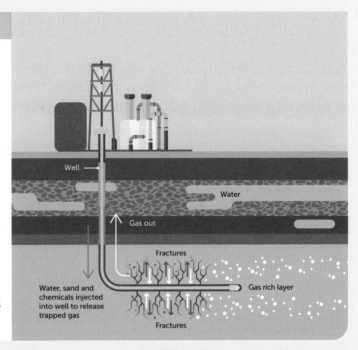

The first shale gas plant in the UK opened in the Bowland Basin in Lancashire. It was drilled briefly, however some small magnitude earthquake events led to a pause to the drilling.

1. Which **one** of the following statements describes an economic cost of natural gas extraction? [1]

   A: Carbon capture technology can be used to offset the pollution.

   B: Gas reserves being found in politically unstable areas.

   C: Increase of jobs in an area with natural gas reserves.

   D: Infrastructure associated with extracting natural gas is expensive.

2. 'Extraction of fossil fuels can bring both advantages and disadvantages.'

   Explain this statement using an example you have studied. [6]

   1. D. [1]

   2. Name of fossil fuel: Natural gas.

   Natural gas can be extracted from the ground through the use of hydraulic fracturing. This method can have advantages economically and environmentally, but it can also have economic and environmental disadvantages. Some of the advantages are that natural gas will provide a wide range of jobs in areas which produce natural gas. This is because many specialist skills are needed in the extraction of these gases, and this can also have a positive economic multiplier effect within an area with other jobs being created to support the new industry. Another advantage is that natural gas is the cleanest fossil fuel and is far better than coal and oil because its CO_2 emissions are lower. However, there are also quite a few disadvantages, economically it is extremely expensive to develop gas extraction facilities. The costs also increase when additional infrastructure is needed to be built to accommodate the industrial development. Environmentally, gas extraction is still fundamentally unsatisfactory, as it contributes towards human enhanced climate change. There is also the risk of pollution to local populations such as groundwater pollution from chemicals used in the process. See mark bands provided on page 179.

A SUSTAINABLE FUTURE FOR ENERGY

A sustainable energy supply will meet the needs of our energy use at the present without compromising the future. This can be achieved through the actions of individuals, businesses and governments.

Sustainable individual energy use and carbon footprints

Energy conservation

A **carbon footprint** is a measurement of the CO_2 equivalent that an individual or organisation is using. Reducing our energy demand, and so carbon footprint, can be achieved by:

Home design and demand reduction

- Greater use of energy efficient technologies and changes in law to increase their use of them in the home and in **home design**.
- Greater use of **off-peak energy**. This means using energy later in the night when fewer people are using it.
- Use of **smart meters** to monitor personal energy usage in homes. This can be used to see what uses the most energy and highlight ways to conserve energy.
- **Financial incentives** from governments will help people access new technologies to help with energy efficiency. The incentives can also be used to help people access small scale renewable schemes.

Technology, workplaces and transport

New technologies are being developed to increase the efficiency of products powered by fossil fuels.

Workplaces can become more sustainable through changes to their policies. This can be through investment in energy efficient technologies, such as light fittings, appliances and heating systems. There is also the possibility of switching to renewable energy. Nando's restaurants have successfully moved to renewable electricity across England, Scotland and Wales.

Energy efficient technologies are typically seen in the **transport sector** with newer models of cars being developed that are lighter and consume less fuel per mile. This has been done with the increased use of carbon fibre instead of steel to decrease the weight of the car. There has also been a large increase in the production of electric or hybrid cars. Hybrid cars use both fossil fuels and electricity.

Define 'energy conservation'. [1]

The prevention of the wasteful use of energy.[1]

CHAMBAMONTERA MICRO-HYDRO SCHEME

An example of a local renewable energy scheme in a LIC

Chambamontera is a rural community found in North West Peru within the Andes.

The population struggles with poverty and hasn't been connected to the electricity grid as the people are spread out over a large area. It has limited development, leaving people depending on subsistence farming to survive. The area has ideal conditions for hydroelectric power, with steep sided valleys, high rainfall and fast flowing rivers.

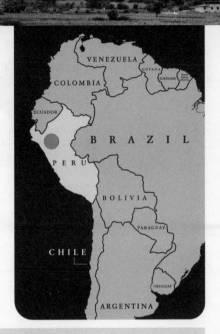

The Chambamontera micro-hydro scheme

The scheme cost $51,000 in total. It was partially funded by the Japanese government, but the rest of the costs needed to be funded by the local population. The cost was $750 per family and credit facilities were set up to fund this. The charity Practical Action supported the project.

Benefits to the community

The community has received a wide range of benefits, **socially**, **economically** and **environmentally**.

Social

- Reduced rural-urban migration as income has increased in the area.
- Improved educational facilities in the area thanks to access to electricity.

Economic

- Low maintenance and running costs for the local community.
- Development of industries such as coffee processing, allowing growth in the local economy.

Environmental

- Reduces the risk of flooding due to regulation of water flow in local rivers.
- Reduced deforestation as local trees are not needed for firewood. This has also reduced soil erosion.

Explain how a local energy scheme in a LIC or NEE is sustainable. [2]

The Chambamontera micro-hydro scheme is sustainable as it uses renewable energy to increase accessibility to energy resources[1] in the remote community in Peru. It has done this through the use of intermediate technology which means that it is affordable and energy efficient for the area.[1]

EXAMINATION PRACTICE

1. Describe **two** issues that may arise from the UK's changing energy mix. [4]

2. Explain the inequalities in food consumption around the world.
   Use your own knowledge and Figure 1 to support your answer. [6]

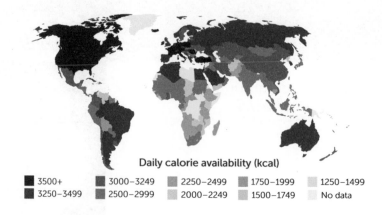

Daily calorie availability (kcal)

■ 3500+	■ 3000–3249	■ 2250–2499	■ 1750–1999	1250–1499
■ 3250–3499	■ 2500–2999	■ 2000–2249	■ 1500–1749	No data

Figure 1

3. Outline **one** advantage of a water transfer scheme in the UK. [2]

4. Name **one** form of renewable energy. [1]

5. Suggest **two** reasons why south east England faces higher water stress than
   north west England. [3]

6. Explain **one** way in which having limited access to food resources can negatively impact
   a country. [2]

7. Outline **one** economic challenge of using non-renewable energy sources. [2]

8. Explain **one** advantage of agribusiness. [2]

9. State what is meant by malnutrition. [1]

10. Discuss the challenges of developing a water transfer system in the UK. [6]

Food option

1. State what is meant by famine. [1]

2. Suggest **two** reasons for countries having different levels of food security. [4]

3. Global demand for food is increasing.

Figure 2a

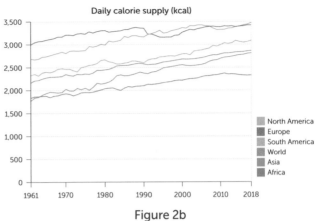

Figure 2b

(a) Explain how food supplies can be made more sustainable using your own understanding and Figures 2a and 2b. [6]

(b) Describe the trends for Europe from the graph in Figure 2b. [2]

(c) Complete the data on average daily calorie consumption in the table below. [3]

Country	1961	2013	Change
China	1,415 kcal	3,108 kcal	
United Kingdom	3,231 kcal		+193 kcal
Afghanistan		2,090 kcal	−909 kcal

(d) Afghanistan had a decrease in average daily calorie consumption between 1961 and 2013. Suggest **one** reason why a country might record a decrease in its daily calorie consumption. [1]

4. Explain how a small scale scheme to improve food supplies you have studied is sustainable. [6]

Name of development: _____

Water option

1. What is meant by water scarcity? [1]

2. Describe the global pattern of domestic water use shown below in Figure 3. [2]

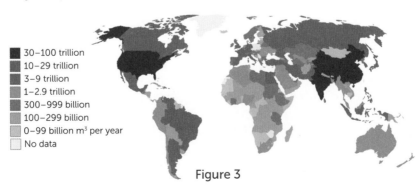

- 30–100 trillion
- 10–29 trillion
- 3–9 trillion
- 1–2.9 trillion
- 300–999 billion
- 100–299 billion
- 0–99 billion m³ per year
- No data

Figure 3

3. Suggest **one** reason why some countries have very high water consumption. [1]

4. Describe how water supplies can be made more sustainable. [2]

5. Outline **one** way in which water demand in an area can decrease. [2]

6. 'A large scale water transfer scheme can bring both advantages and disadvantages.'
    Explain this statement using an example you have studied. [6]
    Name of scheme _____

7. Outline **one** reason why some countries have a limited availability of water. [2]

Energy option

1. Figure 4 shows energy from 1965 to 2019.

    Explain **one** reason for declining energy use in the UK. [2]

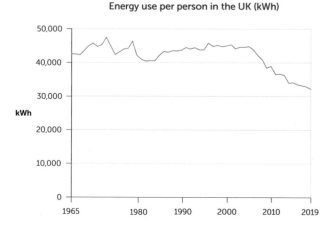

Figure 4

2. State what is meant by energy security. [1]

3. Outline **one** advantage of using renewable sources of energy. [2]

4. Discuss how energy supplies can become more sustainable.
    Use an example of a small scale energy project in your response. [6]

5. Conflict can arise from energy insecurity.
    (a) State **one** other impact of energy insecurity. [1]
    (b) Suggest how issues of energy supply can lead to conflict. [3]

6. Outline **one** way in which economic development leads to increased energy consumption. [2]

TOPICS FOR PAPER 3

Geographical applications

Information about Paper 3

This examination is synoptic – this means that you need to show knowledge, understanding and skills from across the full GCSE course. You will be able to show how well you understand how different areas of geography interrelate.

Written exam: 1 hour 30 minutes
88 marks (including 6 marks for spelling, punctuation, grammar and specialist terminology (SPaG)

Pre-release resources are made available 12 weeks before the exam

30% of qualification grade

Section A: All questions are mandatory (37 marks)

Section B: All questions are mandatory (39 marks)

Specification coverage

Issue evaluation, fieldwork and geographical skills.

Questions

A mix of multiple-choice, short answer and extended-writing questions assessing the application of knowledge, understanding and skills in contextual scenarios.

SECTION A: ISSUE EVALUATION

The first section of Paper 3 is an Issue Evaluation. A pre-release booklet is made available 12 weeks before the examination so that you can prepare for this element. You will be expected to show off your geographical skills and also apply your knowledge.

Pre-release information

A pre-release booklet will include a set of resources focusing on one issue. This issue could be related to:

- The challenge of natural hazards
- The living world
- Urban issues and challenges
- The changing economic world
- The challenge of resource management (core topic only)

> **! Note**
>
> The issue will be synoptic, meaning that you may have to draw on your understanding of several topics. You may also be given resources which are about places you haven't studied (unseen contexts).

When your teacher gives you the resource booklet, you should take time to read it through and think carefully about the issue concerned. You can write notes on the booklet – you will not be able to take this into the exam, but you will be given a new booklet along with the exam paper. The booklet could include:

Maps

Statistics

Satellite images

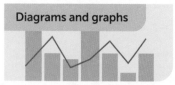
Diagrams and graphs

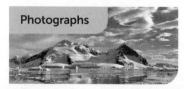
Photographs

Sketches

Extracts from articles or books

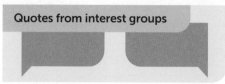
Quotes from interest groups

You will be asked questions relating to the resource booklet and any additional figures in the exam paper. You will need to demonstrate your knowledge in relation to the issue and interpret, analyse and evaluate the information you have been provided with. You will use your geographical skills and will need to consider different viewpoints on the issue.

Think about the main points of views of all stakeholders (people with an interest in the issue). Consider potential options for dealing with the issue. What are the advantages and disadvantages of each? Evaluate each option in comparison to the alternatives.

> ! **Note**
>
> The final question is worth 9 marks – it will ask you to choose **one** option related to the issue and justify your choice. You will need to consider both the impact on people **and** on the physical environment.

Top tips for the issue evaluation section of the examination

- Prepare by carefully **reading** the pre-release resource booklet and **thinking critically** about its content – if you know the resource well, you won't waste time in the exam looking for information.
- **Read questions very carefully** and do exactly as they ask.
- Look out for questions asking you to **complete graphs or diagrams** – these are easy to miss.
- The exam paper will take you through the resources in the pre-release booklet one at a time, then ask a question requiring you to use all of the resources. **Make sure you use the correct resource at the right time**.
- There is likely to be a 6 mark question asking you to **evaluate** a statement or viewpoint. Make sure that you give your opinion, justifying it using evidence from the resource and your own knowledge.
- The 9 mark question will ask you to **choose an option** and **justify** your choice. It is a good idea to say why you chose your option and then add why it is better than the other options.

Look at the example resources on this page, then have a go at answering the questions.

Resource 1

Photograph of the site of West Carclaze Garden Village before development, including the 'Sky Tip'.

> **!** **Note**
>
> The resources in the real pre-release will be much more extensive than this. Look at the AQA website for examples.

Resource 1

Information about West Carclaze Garden Village

West Carclaze Garden Village is one of the first new garden villages to be built in the UK. In 2019, the government announced the plan to build 14 garden villages across the UK.

500 acres of land, some of it previously used for clay mining, on the outskirts of the town of St Austell in Cornwall will be turned into a development of homes within a new country park. There will be leisure spaces, village hubs and public gardens.

The development will use 21st century technology but it will blend with existing communities and the local culture. There will be 1500 homes, 5 lakes, a 210 place primary school, a 7 MW solar park and amenities for local people to use. 450 of the homes will be 'affordable homes'.

Source: https://westcarclaze-gardenvillage.co.uk/

Resource 3

"We don't want this to be some standalone community, we want to be able to serve the people who live nearby in Bugle, Penwithick and St Austell as well. It's not just an enclave."

"We will be opening up all this land that local people haven't been able to go to for some time – some of these areas will be accessible for the first time in more than 100 years."

Chief Development Officer, *West Carclaze Garden Village*

"I think 1500 homes is too many. I don't think there's room for them. There must be green spaces."

Resident
West Carclaze

"30% of the homes on the site will be affordable with another 5% being made available for people who would like to self-build. This is a village, not a housing estate."

Site developer, *Eco-Bos*

"It just seems that for an eco village, it's hardly eco at all compared to what it could be."

"And if we are declaring a climate emergency, then I think it needs to be far more."

Councillor, *St Austell Town Council*

1. Look at Resource 1. Describe the human and physical features of the landscape shown. [3]
2. Look at Resource 2. Discuss the social and environmental benefits that the development of West Carclaze Garden Village could bring for local residents. [6]
3. Look at Resource 3. Give **two** problems identified with the plans for West Carclaze Garden Village. [2]
4. Which of the **three** options below would you support in relation to West Carclaze Garden Village? Justify your choice. Use **all three** resources to answer this question. [9 + 3 SPaG]

Option 1	Option 2	Option 3
The building of West Carclaze Garden Village should go ahead as planned.	The scope of the West Carclaze Garden Village should be reduced so fewer houses are built.	The West Carclaze Garden Village project should be enhanced to make it more sustainable.

1. *Human features shown include the path[1] and the Sky Tip.[1] The main physical feature shown is the vegetation.[1]*

2. *The Garden Village will bring a range of social benefits for local residents, including the opportunity to live in a community in an attractive setting with useful facilities. Children will be able to attend the new school and people on lower incomes will still be able to be part of the community as there will be 450 affordable homes. There will also be environmental benefits as an area once used for clay mining will be turned into a new country park which will provide habitats including five lakes. The 7 MW solar park will mean that the development is powered by renewable energy, reducing emissions of greenhouse gases and the carbon footprint of the development.*

   This answer should be marked using the marking grid for 6 mark questions on page 178. Level 3 – Detailed: 6 marks.

3. *Too many houses[1] and the project not being 'eco' enough.[1]*

4. *The West Carclaze Garden Village project should be enhanced to make it more sustainable. As Resource 1 shows, this is already a site with a striking landscape combining human and physical features, so building houses here should be carefully done so as not to ruin the landscape and habitats.*

   Resource 2 states that some of the land was once used for clay mining, so is brownfield, but this means other parts are using greenfield land. It is admirable that the plans include affordable homes, but these are only 30% of the homes being built. If the development is to be truly sustainable it should meet the needs of the local community, who would benefit from more affordable homes being included.

   As Resource 3 shows, local councillors are concerned that the Garden Village isn't as 'eco' as it could be and that more needs to be done to combat the climate emergency. A local resident highlights the importance of leaving green spaces and says that 1 500 homes are too many for this site.

   The advantage of going ahead with the plan as it is would be a more rapid development of the site, providing much needed homes for people and putting an area of abandoned industrial land back into use. However, slowing down and fully exploring the possibilities of making the site as sustainable as possible could bring greater benefits in the long term.

   Cutting down the number of houses in the plan would reassure local residents, but this could mean the site isn't profitable enough for the developer. I therefore think it is best to take the time to look again at the plans and make them as sustainable as possible.

   This answer should be marked using the marking grid for 9 mark questions on page 179. Level 3 – Detailed: 9 marks.

SECTION B: FIELDWORK

The fieldwork enquiry process

What could you be asked about?

Choosing a geographical question

- What needs to be considered when choosing a question.
- The theory/concept behind the enquiry.
- Where the fieldwork is being carried out (location).
- Sources of primary and secondary evidence.
- What risks may be involved in the fieldwork and how these can be minimised.

Selecting, measuring and recording data

- The difference between primary and secondary data.
- How appropriate data has been identified and selected.
- How data has been measured and recorded using different sampling methods.
- Why certain data collection methods have been used.

Processing and presenting data

- A range of visual, graphical and mapping (cartographic) methods used to present data.
- How to select and accurately use appropriate presentation methods.
- Questions often ask you to complete a graph or map using data provided.

Describing, analysing and explaining data

- Describe, analyse or explain findings.
- Make links between sets of data.
- Use statistical techniques (such as mean, median, mode and range).
- Identify anomalies in data (odd ones out).

Choose a geographical question

↓

Select, measure and record appropriate data

↓

Process and present data in appropriate ways

↓

Describe, analyse and explain the data

↓

Reach conclusions

↓

Evaluate the enquiry

Reaching conclusions

- Draw conclusions supported by evidence.
- Link the conclusions back to the aims of the enquiry.

Evaluation of geographical enquiry

- Identify problems in data collection methods.
- Identify limitations of data collected.
- Suggest other data that would be useful to collect.
- Discuss the extent to which conclusions are reliable.

Unseen fieldwork

You will be asked questions about a fieldwork enquiry carried out by someone else. Information about their fieldwork will be shared with you in the exam paper. You could be asked about any stage of the enquiry process. Questions in this section will often relate to figures and are worth 1–4 marks each.

Study Figure 1, a table showing information collected by students in a coastal town.

Area	Function	Attractiveness /5	Cleanness /5	Safety /5	Total score	Mean score
A	Residential	4	5	5	14	4.6
B	Residential	4	3	2	9	
C	Tourist area	3	3	3	9	3
D	Tourist area	4	5	5	14	4.6

Figure 1

1. Calculate the mean score for area B. [1]

Study Figure 2, a set of photographs of the four areas investigated in the fieldwork.

Figure 2

2. (a) Suggest **one** risk that students may face when visiting this coastal town. [1]

   (b) State **one** action which could be taken to reduce this risk. [1]

A student presented the safety scores given in Figure 1 using the method shown in Figure 3.

3. (a) Suggest a more appropriate way to present the safety scores from Figure 3. [1]

6
5
4
3
2
1
0
Safety score
A
B
C
D
Location

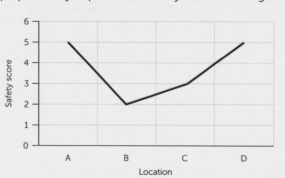

Figure 3

(b) Give **one** reason for your choice. [1]

Study Figure 4, a questionnaire used in areas A–D to find out what people thought of the environment in each place.

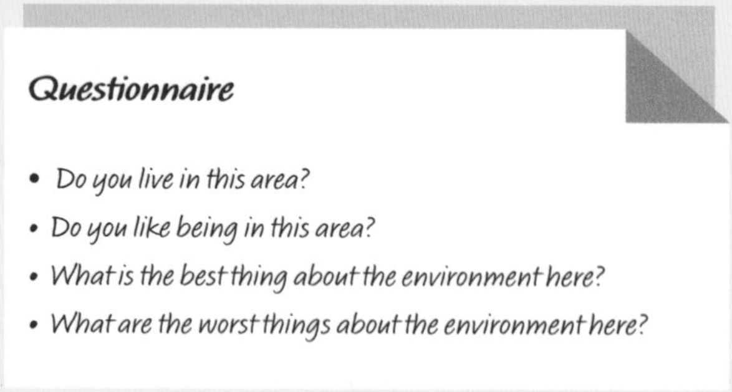

Questionnaire
• Do you live in this area?
• Do you like being in this area?
• What is the best thing about the environment here?
• What are the worst things about the environment here?

Figure 4

4. (a) Suggest **one** additional question that could be added to the questionnaire. [1]

(b) Give **one** reason why your question might provide useful information. [1]

Study Figure 5, a bird's eye view diagram showing a student's transect sites on a beach.

Harbour wall
W
X
Y
Z
North
Predicted direction of sediment movement (longshore drift)

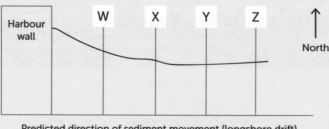

Figure 5

5. (a) State the type of sampling shown in Figure 5. [1]

   (b) Give **one** advantage of using this type of sampling. [1]

Study Figure 6, which shows the average size of 10 pebbles collected using random sampling at sites W–Z along the beach.

Site	W	X	Y	Z
Average pebble size (cm)	6	5	8	4.6

Figure 6

6. Describe the pattern shown in Figure 6. [2]

7. To what extent could the student draw reliable conclusions about whether sediment is moving along the beach from the findings in Figures 5 and 6? [4]

Answers:

1. *3.[1]*

2. *(a) There is a risk of being hit by a car when crossing roads.[1]*

   (b) Students should use crossings where possible.[1]

3. *(a) A bar chart.[1]*

   (b) It is discrete data.[1]

4. *(a) Answer may vary, e.g. "Do you think this area is well looked after?"[1]*

   (b) A well looked after area will have a better environment, so it would be good to ask this.[1]

5. *(a) Systematic sampling.[1]*

   (b) All areas are sampled equally.[1]

6. *The average size of pebbles gets larger as you go from east to west[1] except for site Y, which is an anomaly.[1]*

7. **This question will be marked using levels. An answer achieving full marks could be:**

   The students will be able to draw reliable conclusions to some extent. Their transects will show them how the beach changes from east to west, but using systematic sampling means they have left the same gap between each transect and so may miss out unusual features. Using pebble sampling as well as transects will allow them to compare two different sets of data, making their conclusions more reliable.

   This answer should be marked using the marking grid for 4 mark questions on page 178. Level 2 – Clear: 4 marks.

Your own fieldwork

GCSE geography students carry out **two** enquiries as part of their course. They must:

- Involve collecting primary data during fieldwork
- Be linked to the GCSE specification
- Take place outside the classroom and school site
- Be carried out in contrasting environments
- Show an understanding of both physical and human geography

At least one of the enquiries must include interaction between physical and human geography.

You will need to know the title of your individual enquiry to answer questions in this section of Paper 3. The questions asked could be about any part of the enquiry process.

Questions will clearly state whether you need to answer in relation to your physical enquiry or your human enquiry or if you are able to choose. Read questions carefully and do what they ask.

There are usually questions worth 2, 3, 6 and 9 marks in this part of the exam, with the 9 mark question receiving an additional 3 marks for spelling, punctuation and grammar (SPaG).

1. Write the title of your physical geography enquiry.
    (a) Identify **one** aim of your enquiry and give **one** reason why this was chosen. [2]
    (b) Justify **one** method of data presentation used in your physical geography enquiry. [3]

2. Write the title of your human geography enquiry.
   Assess the suitability of your data collection method(s). [6]

3. For **one** of your fieldwork enquiries, evaluate the reliability of your conclusions
   and suggest how they could be improved. [9] [+3 SPaG marks]

   1. *Title of physical geography enquiry: Is there evidence of longshore drift on Monmouth Beach?*

      (a) *I aimed to find out if the beach got wider from the west to the east.[1] This would show that longshore drift was moving the sand along the beach until it built up by the harbour wall.[1]*

      (b) *I drew profiles to show the width and height of the beach at different points along the coastline.[1] This clearly showed whether the beach got wider[1] and also if longshore drift meant that the sand was building up at the east of the beach, making it higher.[1]*

   2. *Title of human geography enquiry: Is the regeneration of Temple Quarter in Bristol sustainable?*

      When I visited Temple Quarter I carried out bi-polar environmental surveys along a transect to find out about the quality of the environment. This meant that I could compare the regeneration to the Egan Wheel, which says that sustainable communities should have good quality environments. This was useful data to collect, but I only looked at the environment along one transect. I also carried out a land use transect to find out if the economy is thriving, which is another aspect on the Egan Wheel. These were both very useful data collection methods to use.

      This answer should be marked using the marking grid for 6 mark questions on page 178. Level 3 – Detailed: 6 marks.

3. *For my physical enquiry, I concluded that there is evidence of longshore drift at Monmouth beach. This was based on my measurements of the width of the beach which clearly showed that the beach was wider in the east than in the west, suggesting that longshore drift was moving pebbles along the beach until they were stopped by the harbour wall, building up and making the beach wider. This was also shown by my sketches of the east and west ends of the beach. However, my beach profiles didn't show that the beach got steeper at the eastern end, which I was expecting to see as evidence of longshore drift. I also measured pebble size to find out if pebbles nearer the harbour were smaller and rounder, expecting them to have been eroded by attrition as they moved along the beach. The pebble size didn't show any clear pattern along the beach. I am therefore not fully confident that my conclusion is reliable as not all of my data showed evidence of longshore drift. If I studied a longer piece of beach, I might have been able to see more of a change in pebble size, making my conclusions more reliable. I could also improve my enquiry by placing painted pebbles on the beach and observing them to see how they were moved by the waves over a period of time.*

This answer should be marked using the marking grid for 9 mark questions on page 179. Level 3 – Detailed: 9 marks.

GEOGRAPHICAL SKILLS

Use this checklist to make sure you know the geographical skills you are expected to have.

Cartographic (map) skills

✓ Atlas maps

Including coordinates, distribution and patterns of features, different scales, interrelationships between human and physical factors.

Ordnance Survey maps

Including different scales, coordinates, distance and direction, gradient, contours and spot heights, landscape and relief features, cross-sections and transects.

Maps used alongside photographs

Including comparing maps, sketch maps, interpreting photographs, describing landscapes, labelling and annotating diagrams, maps, graphs, sketches and photos.

Examples

Distribution of plate margins **p4**

Biome map **p29**

OS map showing River Tees **p69**

OS maps showing the edge of Bristol **p125**

Interpreting photos **p10**

Topographical map of the UK **p52**

Graphical skills

Examples

Line graph **p20**

Bar graph **p22**

Climate graph **p31**

Hydrograph **p71**

Population pyramids **p105**

Choropleth maps **p127**

Contour lines on OS map **p69**

Interpreting information from a graph **p102**

Choose and draw appropriate graphs and charts to present data

Line charts, bar charts, pie charts, pictograms, histograms with equal class intervals, divided bar, scattergraphs and population pyramids. Suggest which type of graph would be appropriate for data provided.

Interpret and take information from...

...maps, graphs and charts including population pyramids, choropleth maps, flow-line maps and dispersion graphs

Complete graphs and maps...

...choropleth, isoline, dot maps, desire lines, proportional symbols and flow lines.

Use and understand isoline maps

e.g. contour lines – gradient, contour and value.

Plot information on graphs

Where the axes and scales have been provided.

Suggest which type of graph would be appropriate for data provided.

Numerical skills

Identify...
...weaknesses in statistical presentation of data.

Describe data
When there are two variables, add trend lines to scatter plots, draw estimated lines of best fit, make predictions and work out what the key trends are.

Use measures of central tendency, spread and cumulative frequency appropriately
Median, mean, range, quartiles and interquartile range, mode and modal class.

Examples

Average scores for Bristol **p96**   Calculating a mean **p163**

Use of qualitative and quantitative data

Use both **quantitative** (number) and **qualitative** (opinion) data

Obtain, illustrate, communicate, interpret, analyse and evaluate geographical information

Use data from both **primary** and **secondary** sources

Types of data can include maps, fieldwork data, GIS, satellite imagery, written and digital sources and numerical and statistical information

Examples

Different types of data are explored on pages **163–165**.

Formulate enquiry and argument

Identify questions and sequences of enquiry

Describe, analyse and criticise in writing

Communicate ideas effectively

Develop a written argument

Draw conclusions about geographical questions and issues

Literacy

Communicate using **good literacy** skills.

Communicate information in ways suitable for different audiences.

Examples

See fieldwork enquiry process on page **162**.

EXAMINATION PRACTICE

Paper 1   Section A

1. Primary responses happen in the immediate aftermath of an event, whereas secondary responses happen in the weeks, months or years after an event.   [1]

2. D. Warm moist air.   [1]

3. Answers in order: state (1), winds (1), air (1).   [3]

4. Earthquakes.   [1]

5. Indicative content: Discussion around the difference between immediate and secondary impacts. Primary: Buildings collapse (E), infrastructure destroyed (E&V), people killed (Y). Secondary impacts: Tsunami (Y), disease spread (Y), economic decline (Y). This list is not exhaustive. Award credit for other reasonable responses.

    This question should be marked in accordance with the levels-based mark scheme on page 179. Max level 2 if a named example isn't used.

    Example of an answer scoring 9 marks:

    Immediate impacts of a tectonic hazard, such as earthquakes and volcanoes, would happen during or in the immediate aftermath of an event. Examples of immediate impacts will be deaths and damage to roads or infrastructure. In Nepal 2015, immediate impacts included over 9,000 deaths due to the earthquake event, and significant damage to the large parts of Nepal including the capital city Kathmandu.

    Secondary impacts will happen in the days, weeks, months and years after an event has taken place. Examples of secondary impacts could be economic decline and the spread of disease. The Chile earthquake in 2010 had secondary impacts such as large landslides which blocked access to remote regions impacted by the earthquake, as well as a tsunami that devastated some coastal towns.

    Overall, I somewhat agree with the statement. The immediate impacts are often more devastating and destructive, however it depends on the circumstances of the event. For example a tsunami may be more devastating in an area compared to the earthquake.   [9]

6. Weather that is different from the norm. (1) / Weather that can threaten/damage to lives or livelihoods. (1)   [1]

7. Credit any extreme weather case study, e.g., Somerset Levels Flooding (2014), Storm Eunice (2022).   [1]

8. The UK climate can be impacted by several different air masses, each of these air masses brings a different dominating weather type (1). An example of this is the tropical continental air mass which brings hot dry weather in the summer (1).   [2]

9. There is lots of evidence suggesting that UK weather systems are going to become more extreme due to human enhanced climate change, in the UK we can expect heatwaves to become more intense and last longer. (1) This can cause damage to infrastructure, as well as cause deaths to the most vulnerable in society. (1) Another way in which the UK's weather is going to become more extreme is storms and flooding events. (1) These are much more likely to occur, and become more damaging when they do occur, in some areas flood risk has increase upwards of 20%. (1)   [4]

10. *Indicative content:* Social impacts can be anything related to how people have been impacted, such as evacuations, houses flooded, injuries, and deaths. Marks awarded for stating a social impact and then developing the point. Environmental impacts can be anything related to the natural world, such as, pollution, and damaged or destroyed habitats. Named examples are any relevant UK weather event, examples include the Somerset Levels Floods (2014) or the Beast from the East Storm (2016). No credit given for economic answers, unless related to a social impact or environmental impact.

    This question should be marked in accordance with the levels-based mark scheme on page 178.
    Max level 2 if only one social or environmental example is used. Max level 2 if no named example is used.

    Example of an answer scoring 6 marks:

    Extreme weather is any weather that is different from the norm, but can also pose a serious threat to human livelihood. Social impacts are related to how people have been affected by an extreme weather event, and environmental impacts are related to how the natural world has been impacted. The Somerset Levels flood of 2014 had several social and environmental impacts. The social impacts included houses being flooded, which impacted hundreds of people as it meant they couldn't stay in their houses for an extended period of time, and also meant their homes were significantly damaged. An environmental impact of the 2014 Somerset Level floods was that significant areas were left polluted once the flood waters drained away as sewage and chemicals had leached into the flood waters. This requires a lot of cleaning and could have had a major impact on the wildlife in the area.   [6]

11. Naming and explaining one of three natural causes of climate change: Orbital variations (1) – Milankovitch cycles (eccentricity, axial tilt, and precession) cause the distance between Earth's closest and farthest approach around the sun to increase (warming the Earth) or decrease (cooling). This impacts global climate. (1)

Solar output (1) – The sun goes through an 11-year cycle of solar sunspot activity. This causes solar output to increase and decrease causing changes to global climate. (1)

Volcanic activity (1) – Ash from volcanic eruptions and sulphur dioxide can reduce the level of solar energy reaching the surface of the Earth causing global cooling. (1)

Only one cause to be stated. 1 mark maximum if there is no development to the answer. [2]

12. The natural greenhouse effect is when naturally produced gases such as CO_2 and methane help to insulate the planet and retain some solar energy as heat energy. The enhanced greenhouse effect is where additional greenhouse gases are released causing more solar energy to become trapped as heat energy, causing Earth's climate to get warmer. [2]

13. (a) Long term evidence: Ice cores (1), fossil records (1), tree rings (1), sediment records. (1) [1]

(b) Recent evidence: Melting ice caps and glaciers (1), rising sea levels (1), changes in average global temperature (1), changes in global weather patterns. (1) [1]

14. Mitigation means trying to reduce the impacts of change through management, whereas adaptation means changing to live with the impacts. [1]

15. Two developed points needed to access 4 marks. One developed point would allow for 2 marks maximum. Two strategies that are named but not developed, max 2 marks.

This question should be marked in accordance with the levels-based mark scheme on page 178.
Indicative content:
Carbon capture: Remove CO_2 from the atmosphere, compress it and store it in underground wells, such as depleted oil and gas reservoirs.
Planting trees: Trees are a natural carbon sink as they absorb CO_2 during photosynthesis.
International agreements: Governments are working together to set international goals to reduce global warming. Such as the 2015 Paris agreement.
Alternative energy sources: Using renewable energy sources instead of fossil fuels. HEP, solar, nuclear, wind, tidal, are all sustainable, low-carbon energy sources. [4]

16. (a) Destructive / convergent plate boundary. [1]
(b) A. 6 m. [1]

17. Eye wall. [1]

18. Tropical storms do not form on the Equator due to the Coriolis effect, the deflection of air due to the rotation of the Earth (1) being too weak to form a vortex. (1) This is why they are only found above 5 degrees latitude. (1) [2]

19. *1 mark for stating opinion on the statement. (1) 2nd mark for giving a reason. (1)*

Model answer: I disagree with the statement above. This is because you can see that the deaths in the 2010 Haiti Earthquake were significantly higher than the larger magnitude 2011 Tohoku Earthquake and Tsunami. [2]

20. Surface winds form as the sun heats parts of the Earth unevenly, causing areas of high and low pressure. [1] Air moves from an area of high pressure to an area of low pressure. [1] / As warm air rises, it creates lower pressure and more air moves in to that space to replace it, causing wind. [1] [2]

Paper 1   Section B

1. D. There are areas of mixed and deciduous forests in six of the seven continents. [1]

2. Deserts are found in areas with high pressure (1) which are associated with a dry climate (1). [2]

3. 4°C or 25-29°C. [1]

4. August. [1]

5. *This question should be marked in accordance with the levels-based mark scheme on page 179.*
Example of an answer scoring 9 marks:
In the Amazon Rainforest the environmental costs of using the rainforest currently outweigh the economic benefits, but this may not be the case in the future if use of the rainforest is managed sustainably.
Countries which are home to the Amazon are developing rapidly and want to exploit the resources of the forest. Roads such as the Trans-Amazonian Highway have opened up the forest for development, which has brought financial gain but at the cost of deforestation, often by illegal loggers. The Carajas iron ore mine is the largest in the world and provides important raw materials as well as employing 3000 workers, but mining can lead to pollution of rivers, and most economic benefit from Carajas goes to the TNC which owns the mine. Deforestation for infrastructure developments, mineral extraction and farming not only harms the local habitat, it also contributes to the climate emergency. Burning the forests releases the carbon stored in them into the atmosphere, spreading the environmental cost around the world.

However, there are success stories in the Amazon. The Amazon Soy Moratorium has stopped companies buying soy grown on land which is newly deforested. The amount of soy being grown in Brazil has increased, but this soy is being grown on land that has already been deforested. Ecotourism is another success story; at the Napo Wildlife Center, tourists stay in 20 lodges made from natural materials, and the centre is managed and run by the local indigenous people who put all profits back into the community.

If sustainable ways of using the Amazon Rainforest can be successfully scaled up, as has been achieved by the Amazon Soy Moratorium, there is hope that whilst environmental costs currently outweigh economic benefits, this may not always be the case. [9]

Hot deserts option

6.   It is very hot in the day but much colder at night. [1]

7.   *This question should be marked in accordance with the levels-based mark scheme on page 178.*
Example of an answer achieving 6 marks:
In the past, deserts such as the Sahara were often used in unsustainable ways, such as for mass tourism or oil extraction. As tourism grew in Egypt, the Sharm el Sheik resort attracted large numbers of tourists, creating a high demand for water in the dry desert and offering Jeep tours which ripped up the fragile desert ecosystem. This also wasn't sustainable economically as most of the money earned went to the TNCs (Trans-national Corporations) which owned the hotels, not local people. The photograph shows how ecotourism developments in Egypt are more sustainable, with rooms being built with thick walls of local stone and small windows to keep them cool without the need for air conditioning and tourists being encouraged to buy local goods. [6]

8.   Tree roots hold the soil together (1) and when leaf litter is broken down the soil becomes more fertile (1). [2]

9.   Water harvesting collects, stores and uses rainwater to tackle desertification (1) whilst well managed soils are less easy to erode (1). Sand dams are an example of appropriate technology which can reduce the risk of desertification (1). The dams trap sand which stores water when rain falls, reducing water shortages and desertification (1). [2]

Cold environments option

10.   There is less insolation in polar areas due to the latitude and angle of the sun's rays. [1]

11.   *This question should be marked in accordance with the levels-based mark scheme on page 178.*
Example of an answer achieving 6 marks:
The first photograph of Svalbard shows that settlements have been built in this cold environment. This could cause problems if the buildings are built directly on the ground as the permafrost will melt, but if the buildings are raised off the ground the environment won't be damaged, making the settlement more sustainable. The second photograph indicates people crossing the ice on snowmobiles, which aren't a sustainable form of transport at they use fossil fuels and can also damage habitats. A more sustainable mode of transport could use Svalbard reindeer, an indigenous species on the islands. However, this would mean domesticating the reindeer as they are wild animals. [6]

12.   The Trans Alaskan pipeline is above the surface so that it doesn't melt the permafrost (1) or block the migration of animals. (1) [2]

13.   International treaties can commit a range of countries to conserving a cold environment, (1) limiting the activities that take place there. (1) [2]

Paper 1   Section C

Coastal landscapes option

1.   Indicative answers include: longshore drift (1), which occurs when waves hit the beach at an angle. (1) Wind (1) as sand blown by the wind forms sand dunes. (1) [2]
Answers relating to traction, saltation, solution or suspension with development should also be credited. One mark for the main point and one for development.

2.   A cliff // wave cut platform. (1) Allow wave cut notch. (1) [1]

3.   B. Hydraulic action. [1]

4.   Answers could refer to a change in the direction of the coastline, a river mouth or a bay. [1]

5.   *This question should be marked in accordance with the levels-based mark scheme on page 178.*
Example of an answer achieving 4 marks:
Sand dunes form when sand is blown inshore by the wind and meets an obstacle. An embryo dune will form, which may then be stabilised by vegetation such as sea couch grass. Over time, soil will develop on the dune and it will become more stable, meaning more varied vegetation will grow on it.
An annotated diagram could also be used to answer this question or to support a written answer. [4]

6. *This question should be marked in accordance with the levels-based mark scheme on page 178.*

   Example of an answer achieving 6 marks:

   Hard engineering strategies have been effective in protecting the coastline in Burnham on Sea. A large wave return wall was built in 1986 and there has been no flooding since. However, this wall cost £7.5 million, which was too much to justify in the case of the village of Berrow, found to the north of Burnham on Sea. At Berrow, sand dune regeneration has been used, which is a soft engineering strategy and is both much cheaper than a sea wall and more natural. This shows that hard engineering strategies may be more effective in some locations, but in others, soft engineering strategies are equally effective in protecting the coastline. [6]

River landscapes option

1. Abrasion (1), hydraulic action (1) or solution (1) would be correct. Abrasion uses material carried by the river to wear away the bed and banks. Hydraulic action is when the force of the water breaks up and carries away material from the bed and banks. Solution is when weak acid in the river water dissolves the bed and banks if they are made of materials such as limestone.

   Do not credit attrition as this affects the river's load rather than the bed and banks. One mark for the point and one additional mark for development. [2]

2. Indicative answers include the intensity of the rain (1) or the ground being covered in impermeable surfaces. (1) [1]

3. A. Attrition. [1]

4. The flow of water is fastest here (1) so there is more erosion here. (1) [2]

5. *This question should be marked in accordance with the levels-based mark scheme on page 178.*

   Example of an answer achieving 4 marks:

   Waterfalls can form when a river flows from more resistant rock to less resistant rock. The less resistant rock is eroded more rapidly, creating a step in the river. Over time, the less resistant rock will continue to be eroded, forming a plunge pool and undercutting the more resistant rock to form an overhang. When the overhang eventually collapses the waterfall will retreat. *An annotated diagram could also be used to answer this question or to support a written answer.* [4]

6. *See marking grid for 6 mark answers.*

   An answer achieving 6 marks would be:

   Storm hydrographs show the relationship between precipitation and discharge in a river. This means that the precipitation will have a huge influence on the shape of the hydrograph, both in terms of intensity and duration. Other physical factors that play a role include the rock type in the area and the relief. If heavy rain falls on impermeable rock there will be a great deal of runoff, meaning the hydrography will have a short lag time and a high peak. However, human factors can influence hydrographs as the flow of a river may be controlled by a dam, or nearby roads and houses may have created impermeable surfaces. In conclusion, physical factors are most significant, but human factors shouldn't be ignored. [6]

Glacial landscapes option

1. Abrasion (1) or plucking (1). One mark for the point and one for development. Abrasion erodes the landscape when material carried by glaciers wears away the land they are passing over. Plucking erodes the landscape when the glacial ice sticks to the land below and pulls pieces of rock away as it moves. [2]

2. Freeze-thaw. [1]

3. C. Drumlin. [1]

4. Material transported by a glacier. [1]

5. *This question should be marked in accordance with the levels-based mark scheme on page 178.*

   Example of an answer achieving 4 marks:

   Corries form high on valley sides in glaciated areas. As the glacial ice moves in a rotational motion weathered material is plucked from the back of the corrie, whilst the rotational motion abrades the base, creating a hollow in the valley side. If the glacial ice melts a tarn will form in the hollow.
   An annotated diagram could also be used to answer this question or to support a written answer. [4]

6. *This question should be marked in accordance with the levels-based mark scheme on page 178.*

   Example of an answer achieving 6 marks:

   Glaciated upland areas in the UK are often used for farming, tourism, forestry and quarrying. Conflicts can occur between people wanting to use this land in different ways. An example is that the Lake District was visited by over 19 million people in 2018, with many of these people taking walks across the countryside. Sheep farms in the Lake District can suffer from disruption if walkers forget to close gates or don't keep their dogs on leads. Quarrying can also cause conflict with tourism as quarries can cause damage to the landscape, increase traffic, create loud noises and dust which is unpleasant for tourists. Local residents may become frustrated with tourists as they can cause traffic congestion, and the large number of holiday homes in places like the Lake District forces up house prices out of the reach of locals. [6]

Additional question

Coastal landscapes: The photograph shows an arch and a stump which were created by a combination of weathering and erosion. Caves form when coastal erosion widens and deepens a crack in the cliff through physical processes such as hydraulic action and abrasion. If the cave is on a headland, it may eventually erode through the headland, forming an arch. Over time, erosion will make the arch wider, but weathering will also break down the roof of the arch. Eventually the roof of the arch will collapse, leaving a stack, which will then be eroded to form a stump like the one shown.

River landscapes: The photograph shows a waterfall and its gorge. Waterfalls often form when a river flows from a more resistant rock to a less resistant rock. The force of the falling water wears away the less resistant rock (hydraulic action), cutting it back and leaving the more resistant rock as an overhang. A plunge pool is formed at the base of the waterfall as the water erodes the river bed. Eventually the overhang will collapse and the waterfall will retreat, leaving a steep sided gorge behind.

Glacial landscapes: The photograph shows a range of landforms, including an arête and a corrie. Corries form when glacial ice builds up on a mountainside and starts to flow down the mountain due to gravity. The ice will erode the mountainside through plucking and abrasion, forming a hollow in the mountainside. Plucking occurs when the ice sticks to the rock and pulls pieces away whereas abrasion is caused when rocks carried by the ice wear the rock away like sandpaper. If two corries cut back towards each other, they form a sharp ridge called an arête. When the glacial ice melts, a landscape like the one in the photograph is revealed.

Paper 2 — Section A

1. C. [1]

2. Little (1), urbanisation (1), 1990 (1). [3]

3. Answers should give two reasons – one mark per reason. Reasons could be fear of conflict, looking for a new home, lack of food, wanting a better life for children or any other answer linked to the article. [2]

4. Answers should give one problem related to the economy and then develop the point to gain the second mark. Example: The tourist bus is stuck in the traffic jam which might put people off visiting London (1) which would reduce the amount of money being spent in the city (1). [2]

5. *See marking grid for 6 mark answers. An answer achieving 6 marks would be:*
    The photograph shows traffic congestion in London, which will also lead to air pollution as exhaust fumes contain carbon dioxide, particles and other pollutants. Air pollution is also a significant environmental challenge in Bristol, but both cities are tackling it by promoting public transport, so it may be less of a problem in the future. The growth of Bristol has also led to major problems with waste disposal, particularly food waste. This is being tackled by the #SlimMyWaste project and the waste is being processed to fuel bio buses as part of Bristol's ITS. [6]

6. (a) Percentage increase = 100 × (51.2 − 126.2 / 51.2) = 146.5% [1]
    (b) See marking grid for 4 mark answers. An answer achieving 4 marks would be:
    The table shows that there are inequalities in health between Filwood and Clifton, with a six year difference in male life expectancy. This could be because people in Filwood live in a comparatively deprived area, with less money to make sure they have a good diet and access to exercise. People in Clifton are more likely to be economically active than people in Filwood, which could be linked to the higher GCSE scores in Clifton as it is easier for people to get jobs if they have better qualifications. [4]

7. Answers should give one pull factor and then develop the point to gain the second mark. Example: A wider range of employment opportunities may attract people from rural areas to cities (1) as they will be able to earn more money and so improve their quality of life (1). [2]

8. *See marking grid for 9 mark answers. An answer achieving 9 marks and 3 marks for SPAG would be:* [9]+[3]
    Lagos is a city on the coast in Nigeria, which is a NEE. Lagos had a population of nearly 15 million in 2021, an increase of 3.44% from 2020. This growth has brought significant challenges, including pressure on housing and the environment. Some of these challenges are being tackled, but others show little improvement.

    60% of people in Lagos can't afford good quality housing, so live in areas such as Mokoko, where houses are often damp and there is a constant risk of eviction. However, the Nigerian Slum/Informal Settlement Federation supports people in improving their housing and access to water supplies and the Lagos Rent to Own scheme means more people are moving into good quality housing as they can put down a 5% deposit and then pay the rest over 10 years.

    Most homes in Lagos have access to electricity, but this may be unreliable and often comes from diesel generators which cause air pollution and so health problems. Air pollution caused 11 200 premature deaths in Lagos in 2018. The World Bank is working with organisations in Lagos to encourage more use of public transport and some areas are moving towards use of solar lighting.

    Many people have moved to Lagos for jobs, but 65% of Lagosians work in the informal sector, so have no job security. There are also problems with poor funding of schools, meaning low levels of education and making it hard for children to gain formal jobs. These are areas in which little improvement is evident.

    Therefore, I conclude that urban change in Lagos has meant challenges to a great extent, but with political will, these challenges can be tackled.

1. Answers could make two points or one developed point. Example: Countries with the highest HDI of over 0.8 are usually found in higher latitudes (1), with large numbers in North America, Europe and Oceania. (1)   [2]

2. Answers should make three relevant points. Limitations of GDP, such as it being an economic indicator (1) and so only looking at wealth and not social indicators. (1) Benefits of HDI such as it being an index which combines economic and social indicators (1) so gives a more balanced picture of the development of a country. (1)   [3]

3. Answers should give one physical factor and then develop the point to gain the second mark. Example: Mountains (1) can cause a barrier which can limit trade and so restrict development, but the barrier can also protect a country from attack and so benefit development. (1)   [2]

4. *See marking grid on page 178 for 4 mark answers. An answer achieving 4 marks would be:* Debt relief means that some debts owed by a country are dropped, meaning that money that would have been spent on debt payments can be spent on developing the country by investment in industry to provide jobs or in public services to improve access to education and healthcare. In 2005 the G8 voted to drop the debts of the poorest countries and by 2015, 36 countries had debts to the IMF cancelled, meaning US$75 billion could be spent on projects to boost development.   [4]

5. (a) B.   [1]
   (b) C.   [1]
   (c) D.   [1]

6. *See marking grid on page 178 for 4 mark answers. An answer achieving 4 marks would be:* Businesses would benefit from being close to the junction with the M4 and M5 motorways so that people could get to work and deliveries could be made. The Aztec West site is on the edge of the city and so there is plenty of space for large buildings and landscaped grounds. The businesses could work on collaborative projects with each other and would also benefit from the retail centre and hotel.   [4]

7. *See marking grid on page 178 for 6 mark answers. An answer achieving 6 marks would be:*
   Cambridge Science Park is an example of a modern industrial development which is trying to be more environmentally sustainable. Smart paving is being used to absorb nitrogen dioxide, turning it into harmless nitrates which are washed away by rain, tackling pollution. The green spaces include trees and lakes, providing a range of habitats to support biodiversity. Some older buildings no longer meet sustainability standards so these are being replaced with new buildings which will minimise energy use and carbon emissions, contributing to a sustainable future.   [6]

8. *See marking grid on page 179 for 9 mark answers. An answer achieving 9 marks would be:*
   Economic changes have led to depopulation in some rural areas, such as Powys in mid Wales. An average of 1000 young people were leaving each year in the run up to 2019, leading to school closures due to a lack of demand and reduced services due to budget cuts. The loss of young people has led to an ageing population in Powys and the council is keen to keep young people in the area by making improvements to education, opportunities and infrastructure.
   In contrast, the population of South Cambridgeshire is growing rapidly, with 8.8% growth from 2018 to 2019. People moving into the area have increased the demand for housing, pushing prices well above the UK average and making it difficult for local people to buy their own homes. Businesses may benefit from more customers for their businesses, but others are worried that their rural villages are becoming suburbanised and their character is changing. Demand for new housing is also leading to greenfield housing development which removes habitats and increases the urbanised area.
   In conclusion, the impact of economic changes on rural landscapes in the UK has been significant, whether the rural area is seeing depopulation or rapid growth. Depopulation brings social challenges such as an ageing population and reduced services, whilst population growth can threaten both the environment and the chances of local people affording a home.   [9]

1. Some people are concerned about the reliability of renewable energy. Sources such as wind and solar energy are dependent on the weather and climate. If there was an over reliance on these sources then UK energy could be less secure. Other sources such as nuclear energy are incredibly expensive to build and develop and can't fix immediate energy needs.   [4]

2. Availability is linked with consumption. The region with the lowest calorie availability is Sub Saharan Africa. This could be linked to the climate. In this area of the world it is much more arid, which means that water may not be available for growing crops and this could cause increased food insecurity. The areas of the world with the highest calorie consumption are in North America and Europe. These areas are the most economically developed, and this means they can afford to import food when they need, but they also use more advanced technology to make productivity within agriculture higher, and therefore increasing food security. Overall food consumption is typically higher in countries that are more developed.   [6]

3. Water transfer would help areas in the UK with a water deficit get greater access to water from areas of water surplus (1), for example, by transferring reserves from NW England to East Anglia. (1)   [2]

4. Answers may include: wind, solar, wave, tidal, biomass and geothermal. Any other reasonable answer will be accepted.   [1]

5. South east England has a much higher population than north west England, this means that the demand for water is much higher (1). North west England also has a water surplus, whereas the south east has a water deficit (1). This is due to the climate being drier in the south east than the north west (1). [3]

6. Limited food resources can lead to a country's population becoming malnourished. (1) This happens when the daily consumption of food is far below what is needed and leads to a variety of health issues. (1) [2]

7. Non-renewable sources of energy can be very expensive to develop (1) as they require a lot of infrastructure, such as roads, pipelines and storage facilities. (1) [2]

8. Agribusiness will increase agriculture in an area (1), increasing food security. (1) [2]

9. Malnutrition is a lack of nutrition through not having enough food or the right food to eat. [1]

10. A water transfer scheme moves water from one part of an area to another. In the UK this would mean moving water from an area of water surplus, (an area with water supplies that are higher than demand), to an area of water deficit, (an area where demand is higher than the supply). This would be very challenging economically as a scheme of this scale would be extremely expensive. It would require a lot of new infrastructure to be built, such as canals and pipelines. People may also be opposed to the development of a water transfer scheme as the money spent on the scheme could be used to invest in more efficient technology to ensure that water isn't being wasted in the areas that need it most. Environmentally there would also be costs, as a water transfer system of this scale would likely disturb ecosystems during the building of the infrastructure needed. Overall, there are a lot of associated challenges with developing a water transfer scheme in the UK.
   Mark band 3: 6 marks. [6]

Food option

1. Extreme scarcity of food. [1]

2. Climate. [1] Some countries have more arid climates which means that growing food may be more difficult as water supplies may be limited and therefore food security threatened. [1]

   Technology. [1] Some countries have poor access to technology that makes agriculture efficient, this means that they will produce less food and reduce their food security. [1]

   Pests and diseases. [1] Tropical regions are more likely to be impacted from pests and diseases. This means that crops and livestock could be impacted and reduce the quantity and/or quality of food. [1]

   Water stress. [1] Some regions suffer from water stress/scarcity and this means that crops are more likely to fail. This is common in arid environments. [1]

   Conflict. [1] Conflict will destabilise a country. This might mean they will be less likely to import staple foods, or less likely to be able to produce foods as crops are, or agricultural land is destroyed by conflict. [1]

   Poverty. [1] This means that the local populations may not be able to afford to import food or be able to afford a regular supply of food. This decreases the food security of an area. [1]

   One mark for each of two relevant answers plus one mark for a development point for each response. [4]

3. (a) *Indicative response:*
   Sustainability means to meet the needs of the present without compromising the future. One method of food production that meets these criteria is organic farming. This is the process of farming without the use of artificial chemicals or manmade fertilisers. This is sustainable because it limits the pollution that is produced when chemicals are used in agriculture. Another method of sustainable food production is urban farming as shown in Figure 2a. This is where produce is grown in urban areas, often in derelict or run down areas. This is sustainable as it allows people to be educated on how to grow crops, it lowers the food miles of the produce grown and also requires a community approach. [6]

   (b) In Europe in the period 1961–1980 there was a steady rise before stagnating [1]. In the 1990s there was a significant drop before starting to increase from 2000 onwards [1]. [2]

   (c) [3]

Country	1961	2013	Change
China	1415 kcal	3108 kcal	**+1693 kcal**
United Kingdom	3231 kcal	**3424 kcal**	+193 kcal
Afghanistan	**2999 kcal**	2090 kcal	−909 kcal

   (d) Conflict between countries could cause their food security to decrease.
   Credit any reasonable response. [1]

4. Name of development: Sand dams in Kenya.

The sand dams in Kenya are an example of a sustainable approach to increasing food supply in an area. They are small concrete dams built across ephemeral rivers (rivers that only have water in them seasonally). The concrete barriers trap sand behind them, the sand is then used as an aquifer to keep the water in place and protect it from evaporation. Increasing the supply of water available to farmers in an area with ephemeral rivers should improve yields and food supplies. This is a sustainable approach using an intermediate technology. Local populations will be able to access the dams and be able to maintain them. Sand dams are also sustainable as they will help alter the microclimate in the area and hopefully this will enable more crops to be grown, increasing food security further. [6]

Water option

1. Having below 1000 m³ of water per person per year. *Answers referring to a lack of water in an area will be accepted.* [1]

2. HICs and NEEs typically have a higher rate of water consumption (1). Countries in Sub-Saharan Africa typically have a lower rate of consumption [1]. Countries with a higher population typically have higher water consumption (1). [2]

3. Some countries may have a very large population and are therefore likely to have a higher rate of water consumption (1). In some developing economies a growing industrial sector might also cause an increase in water consumption (1). [1]

4. Grey water systems can be installed in a home or a business to reuse water for irrigating a garden or crops (1). This means that freshwater isn't wasted (1). [2]

5. Diverting water and increasing storage (1) – Water can be moved from aquifers and reservoirs into storage systems to increase water supply (1).

Dams and reservoirs (1) – Dams are large structures which hold a large volume of water behind them as reservoirs. This means water can be released during drier spells to replenish supplies (1).

Water transfers (1) – These are large infrastructure projects where water is moved from areas of water surplus to areas of water deficit through a series of canals (1).

Desalination (1) –This is where salt is removed from sea water to help increase the supplies of freshwater (1). [2]

6. Name of scheme: Indus Basin Irrigation System.

The Indus Basin Irrigation System (IBIS) spans the length of the Indus River, with the bulk of the irrigation system being in Pakistan. The system helps provide water to the agricultural lands in the south of Pakistan. The system has brought many advantages, such as helping to increase productivity of agriculture in Pakistan and helping to increase food security. The water can also be used to develop fisheries. This has helped diversify the diets of local residents as they now have a new protein to eat. However, the scheme also has many disadvantages, such as some farmers taking an unfair share of the water leaving those further downstream with less of a supply. Local farmers often use inefficient techniques leading to water being wasted. There are also issues as the maintenance of the dams and canals is extremely expensive. Pakistan is a LIC, and this means that maintenance might fall behind and lead to further inefficiency of the system. [6]

7. Climate. (1) Some countries have a much more arid climate which therefore reduces the water availability. (1)

Pollution. (1) Poor sewage and sanitation systems can lead to water supplies being contaminated. (1)

Poverty. (1) Some areas have availability of water, but they can't access the supplies due to not being able to invest in abstracting it. (1) *Accept one answer plus one development point.* [2]

Energy option

1. Energy use may have declined in the UK due to more people using energy efficient technologies [1]. These technologies will use less energy therefore this will decrease consumption. [1]

2. Energy security is the uninterrupted availability of energy sources at an affordable price. [1]

3. A reduced carbon footprint from using renewables [1] helps reduce the rate of human enhanced climate change. [1]

4. Sustainability is when the needs of the present are being met without compromising the future. Energy supplies can be sustainable, but current supplies are not sustainable due to a reliance on non-renewable sources. Renewable energy sources being used more commonly will help increase sustainability as it reduces the carbon footprint of energy sources. The Chambamontera Micro-Hydro Scheme in Peru is an example of a small scale sustainable scheme. This scheme uses hydro-electric power to provide electricity to a small community allowing them to further develop. Sustainability can also be achieved through the use of energy efficient technologies, these help make sure that energy isn't being wasted.
Max Level one for large scale or unsustainable strategies.

5. (a) One from: Decrease in food production [1], decrease in industrial output [1], decrease in population, increase in efficiency of water use.

   (b) Conflicts can arise when energy supplies are not affordable for the majority of the population, causing tensions to rise [1]. International conflicts occur when a country uses its supply of energy to control countries that are dependent on the supply [1]. Tensions can also rise when energy industries are being affected, threatening the jobs of workers [1].

6. As a country undergoes economic development, it increases the access to different technologies in all sectors of the economy [1]. As access is increased, more energy will be consumed in an area. [1]

LEVELS BASED MARK SCHEME FOR EXTENDED RESPONSE QUESTIONS

Questions that require extended writing use mark bands. The whole answer will be marked together to determine which mark band it fits into and which mark should be awarded within the mark band.

4 mark Questions:

Mark Band 2 **Mid Level** **3–4 marks**	• AO1 – Demonstrates accurate knowledge of the geographical topic concerned. • AO2 – Shows a clear understanding of the issue. Explanations are developed.
Mark Band 1 **Low Level** **1–2 marks**	• AO1 – Demonstrates limited knowledge of the geographical topic concerned. • AO2 – Demonstrates limited understanding of the issue. Explanations are partial.
0 marks	• No answer has been given or the answer given is not worth any marks.

6 mark Questions – Assessment objectives assessed will depend upon the question asked:

Mark Band 3 **High Level** **5–6 marks**	• AO2 – Shows thorough understanding of relevant processes or concepts. • AO3 – Demonstrates coherent application of knowledge and understanding in analysis. • AO4 – Relevant reference made to information shown in given figures.
Mark Band 2 **Mid Level** **3–4 marks**	• AO2 – Shows some understanding of relevant processes or concepts. • AO3 – Demonstrates reasonable application of knowledge and understanding in analysis. • AO4 – Some reference made to information shown in any figures present.
Mark Band 1 **Low Level** **1–2 marks**	• AO2 – Shows limited understanding of relevant processes or concepts. • AO3 – Demonstrates limited application of knowledge and understanding in analysis. • AO4 – Limited or partial reference made to information shown.
0 marks	• No answer has been given or the answer given is not worth any marks.

The above descriptors have been written in simple language to give an indication of the expectations of each mark band. See the AQA website for the official mark schemes used.

9 mark Questions:

Mark Band 3		
High Level 7–9 marks	•	AO1 – Demonstrates detailed knowledge with good use of exemplification
	•	AO2 – Shows thorough geographical understanding of places, environments and processes
	•	AO3 – Demonstrates application of knowledge and understanding in a reasoned way when evaluating, using source (if present) and example.
Mark Band 2		
Mid Level 4–6 marks	•	AO1 – Demonstrates clear knowledge with some use of exemplification
	•	AO2 – Shows some understanding of places, environments and processes
	•	AO3 – Demonstrates reasonable application of knowledge and understanding when evaluating, using source (if present) and/or example.
Mark Band 1		
Low Level 1–3 marks	•	AO1 – Demonstrates limited knowledge with little or no exemplification
	•	AO2 – Shows slight understanding of places, environments and processes
	•	AO3 – Demonstrates limited application of knowledge and understanding when evaluating, using source (if present) and/or example (if required).
0 marks	•	No answer has been given or the answer given is not worth any marks.

COMMAND WORDS

Command word	What you need to do
Assess	Make an informed judgement.
Calculate	Work out the value of something.
Compare	Identify similarities and differences.
Complete	Finish the task by adding given information.
Describe	Set out characteristics.
Discuss	Present key points about different ideas or strengths and weaknesses of an idea.
Evaluate	Judge from available evidence, weighing up both sides of an argument.
Explain	Set out purposes or reasons.
Give	Produce an answer from recall.
Identify	Name or otherwise characterise.
Justify	Support a case with evidence.
Outline	Set out main characteristics.
State	Express in clear terms.
Suggest	Present a possible case.
To what extent	Judge the importance or success of (strategy, scheme, project).
Use evidence to support this statement	Select and present information to prove or disprove something.

INDEX

A

abiotic components 28
abrasion 54, 65
adaptations
  in cold environments 45
  in hot deserts 43
  in tropical rainforests 32
aeroponics 134
agribusiness 128
aid 110
Amazon rainforest 34
appropriate technology 138
arch 57, 59
aretes 76
aridisols 37
asthenosphere 3
atmospheric circulation 13
attrition 54, 65

B

backwash 53
balance of trade 109
bars (sand) 58
basal slip 74
bays 57
beaches 58
bilateral aid 110, 117
biodiversity
  of cold environments 45
  of hot deserts 37
  of tropical rainforests 30
biomass 149
biomes 29
biotechnology 134
biotic components 28
birth and death rates 105
boulder clay 75
Bristol 93
  Temple Quarter 98
brownfield sites 97
Burnham on Sea 62
business parks 119
buttress root 30

C

Cadair Idris 77
calorie intake 131
Cambridge Science Park 120
camouflage 32
canopy 30
carbon footprint 152
caves 57
Chambamontera scheme 153
China South-North Project 143
choropleth map 92
climate
  adapting to 25
  causes 23
  change 15
  evidence for 22
  managing 24
  mitigating 24
coastal
  landforms 56
  landscapes 53
  management 60
  processes 54
  realignment 61
cold environments 44
  adaptations 45
  characteristics 44
  economic development 48
  interdependence 44
  Svalbard 46
Commonwealth 124
commuter settlements 97
conservation of water 144
conservative plate margin 5
constructive plate margin 5
convection currents 3
corries 76
crust 3
cyclones 14

D

debt relief 111
decomposers 28
deforestation 33, 35, 70
deindustrialisation 118, 123

Demographic Transition Model
  (DTM) 105
depopulation 121
deposition 55, 65, 66, 75
  glacial 76, 77
  landforms of 58
desalination 142
desertification 40
destructive plate margin 5
diurnal variation 37
drainage basin 64
drip tips 32
dunes 58, 59
  regeneration 61

E

Earth
  core 3
  crust 3
  mantle 3
  plates 4
  structure 3
  effects 6
  responses 6
earthquakes 2, 4, 12
  Chile (HIC) 6
  distribution of 4
  Nepal (LIC) 7
economic
  change 118
  development 87, 104
  migration 121
ecosystems 28
ecotourism 38
emergent layer 30
energy 127
  conservation 152
  consumption 146
  exploitation 130
  global demand 146
  insecurity 148
  in the UK 130
  mix 130
  non-renewable 149
  renewable 149
  security 130
  supply 147, 149

EXAMINATION TIPS

When you practise examination questions, work out your approximate grade using the following table. This table has been produced using a rounded average of past examination series for this GCSE.

Be aware that actual boundaries will vary by a few percentage points either side of those shown.

Grade	9	8	7	6	5	4	3	2	1
Boundary	72%	63%	57%	49%	42%	35%	26%	16%	7%

1. Make sure you know the command words that come up in this exam so that you can respond appropriately. See page 179.

2. Think about how much detail you need to include for different types of question. Use chains of reasoning to develop your statements for questions that ask you to explain or evaluate. Use linking terms such as 'as a consequence...', 'because...' and 'this means that...'.

3. If a source is provided for a question, you are expected to use it. This demonstrates your ability to extract information.

4. If the question says to use a source 'and your own understanding' you need to use the figure provided and support the answer with your own knowledge. You could use an example.

5. Write answers to 6 and 9 mark questions using paragraphs and end them with a clear conclusion. To reach level 3, you will need to answer in detail, supporting your answer with information from any figures and from your examples or case studies.

6. Make sure you know what all the words in the specification mean – it is a good idea to make a list of key terms and their definitions.

7. Questions about formation of landforms require knowledge of specific processes and the sequence of formation. Take care to use the correct geographical terminology.

8. Read questions carefully and do as they ask. You could BUG the question – **B**ox the command word, **U**nderline the key words and then **G**lance over the whole question to check you have understood it.

9. Remember that 10% of the marks in GCSE geography come from mathematical skills. Check that you can use all of the skills listed in the skills checklist on page 168.

10. Check for gaps in your vocabulary and knowledge. You can't access all the marks unless you are secure in your knowledge of terms and concepts. Use regular self-quizzing to find and then fill gaps.

Good luck!

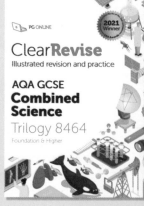

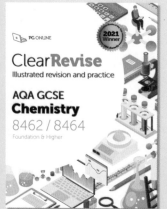
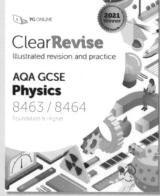